Islands of Voices

The Selected Poems

of

Douglas Oliver

BY DOUGLAS OLIVER:

POETRY
Oppo Hectic (Ferry Press, 1969)
The Harmless Building (Grosseteste and Ferry Presses, 1973)
In the Cave of Suicession (Street Editions, 1974)
The Diagram Poems (Ferry Press, 1979)
The Infant and the Pearl (Silver Hounds, for Ferry Press, 1985)
Kind: Collected Poems (Allardyce, Barnett, Publishers, 1987)
Three Variations on the Theme of Harm (Paladin, 1990)
The Scarlet Cabinet, with Alice Notley (Scarlet Editions, NY, 1992)
Penniless Politics (Bloodaxe Books, 1994)
Penguin Modern Poets 10, with Denise Riley & Iain Sinclair (Penguin, 1996)
Selected Poems (Talisman House, 1996)
etruscan reader viii, with Tina Darragh & Randolph Healy (etruscan books, 1998)
A Salvo for Africa (Bloodaxe Books, 2000)
'27 Uncollected Poems' in *A Meeting for Douglas Oliver*, edited by Wendy Mulford and Peter Riley (infernal methods, Street Editions and Poetical Histories, 2002)
Arrondissements (Salt Publishing, 2003)

PROSE
The Harmless Building (Grosseteste and Ferry Presses, 1973)
Whisper 'Louise' (Reality Street Editions, 2005)

CRITICISM
Poetry and Narrative in Performance (Macmillan/St Martin's Press, 1989)

Islands of Voices

Selected Poems

Douglas Oliver

edited by Ian Brinton
with a Preface by Joe Luna

Shearsman Books

First published in the United Kingdom in 2020 by
Shearsman Books Ltd
PO Box 4239
Swindon
SN3 9FN

Shearsman Books Ltd Registered Office
30–31 St. James Place, Mangotsfield, Bristol BS16 9JB
(this address not for correspondence)

ISBN 978-1-84861-717-9

Copyright © the Estate of Douglas Oliver, 2020
Introduction copyright © Ian Brinton, 2020
Preface copyright © Joe Luna, 2020

The right of Douglas Oliver to be identified as the author of this work has been asserted by his Estate in accordance with the Copyrights, Designs and Patents Act of 1988.
All rights reserved.

Acknowledgements

The publisher is indebted to Alice Notley, widow of Douglas Oliver, and to Neil Astley of Bloodaxe Books for assistance provided in the preparation of this volume.

Contents

Preface	8
Introduction	11

Oppo Hectic

When I Was in Bridport	17
The earthen stairs	18
The Furnaces	19
Oppo Hectic	20
Ordnance Survey Map 178	21
All those factories with offices in the roof girders	22
Mongol in the woods	23
How long anything lasts	24
The Context of the War	26

The Diagram Poems

Team Leader	31
P.C.	33
The Fire Station	36
Central	38
Arrest	41
Gold	43
U	45
The Diagonal Is Diagonal	48

The Infant and the Pearl

	51

An Island That Is All The World

The innermost voyager	95
The Oracle of the Drowned	97
Beyond active and passive	101
The Heron	103
Leaving home island	106
The islands of voices	108
For Kind	110

Penniless Politics   111

A Salvo for Africa

  Our Family Is Full of Problems   141
  The Borrowed Bow   143
  The Childhood Map   144
  The New Medicine   145
  The Toe of a Continent   146
  Well of Sorrows in Purple Tinctures   150

Arrondissements

  The Shattered Crystal
    A Little Night   157
    The Weekend Curfew   158
    Evening Descending Mauve:
        Gisèle Celan-Lestrange   160
    Crystal Eagle 1   161
    Light in Back   162
    From rue d'Enfer to rue Bleue Again   163

  China Blue
    Chinese Bridport   165
    Money in Sunshine   165
    Calling Them Home   166
    Transcending the Hypermarket   167
    Fidelity   167
    East-West Apartments   168
    Puppets in the Butter Chaumont   169
    Chateau Noir   170

Notes   173

for Alice Notley

Preface

This selection of the poetry of Douglas Oliver (1937–2000), with extracts from his prose, draws on works that span the breadth of his writing career, from his first book, *Oppo Hectic* (1969), to the unfinished and posthumously published *Arrondissements*. It is an extraordinary body of work. There is nothing in Anglophone poetry of the second half of the twentieth century quite like it, and it is a testament to the singularity of Oliver's achievement that any attempt to preface a selection such as this one must contend with the dynamic contradictions of the work's motivating principles and formal inheritances, its cross-pollination of a modernist legacy, sceptically but rigorously re-purposed, with equal parts romantic, anarcho-revolutionary idealism, a pragmatic, essentially conservative, democratic humanism, and the transcendental phenomenology of Edmund Husserl, to name just a few essential currents. And yet even such a necessarily broad indication of Oliver's joyously magpie approach to the raw materials of his poetic vocation risks subsuming or obscuring that vocation beneath historical and theoretical commitments which were, for Oliver, always secondary to what he thought of as the central coincidence of poetical form and political life, the speculative identity of which is worked out and through most urgently in the major mature works, *The Diagram--Poems* (1979), *The Infant and the Pearl* (1985), both included here in full, and *Penniless Politics* (1994).

Poetry and any politics worth the name both begin, for Oliver, with the assertion of a radical un-knowledge from which the immediacy of moral purpose may spring, and which lays the foundation of a universalism that draws on a modernist, Poundian system of poetical contribution to what political reality is or should be, even as it relentlessly militates against the equally Poundian, wilfully fetishized intellectualism of high modernism and its contempt for the stupidity of the public. A journalist by occupation for much of his life, Oliver never lost sight of the means by which poetry could, and should, speak to political and social reality from a position of steady, authorial responsibility, a vision which lends to the poetry a demotic precision that maintains and intensifies, rather than jettisons, the shining, reckless ideal of a common humanity. This is a political dialectic of moral culpability, to which the poet as an agent of historical documentation and subjective transfiguration must submit himself, wholly inculcated, wholly a part of the transformation thus sought; it is why great swathes of the poetry rely formally and narratively on the presence of a deeply fallible, semi-autobiographical persona, why

Oliver modelled the biographical interventions into his *oeuvre* on the examples of Dante's *La Vita Nuova* and Coleridge's *Biographia Literaria*, and, crucially, why Oliver made his real-life son, Tom, a central figure in a number of poems and sequences, including the entirety of *The Diagram Poems* and *The Infant and the Pearl*.

Tom, who had Down's syndrome, died in his cot in November 1969. For Oliver he became, in his disability and his infant innocence, a symbol for the pacifist ideal of goodness that plays a vital role in the poetry's emblematic working through of political responsibility and moral courage. Tom is persistently referred to in Oliver's writing by the racist epithets "mongol" or "mongoloid." Whilst Oliver made no excuses for this usage (though he did, in his autobiographical writings, acknowledge its offensiveness), the contexts supplied by the selection of his work in this volume, as well as those outside its scope (including the entire novel *The Harmless Building* (1973) and the grief-stricken, oracular fantasy *In the Cave of Suiccession* (1974)), make plain that its painful, pejorative usage is itself a part of Oliver's vocabulary of coming to terms with moral and personal inadequacy as a foundation of sufficient political will and responsibility. The inadequacy I mean here is Oliver's own: it is by referring to the object of his love and mourning in such terms that Oliver attempts to make the nominally contemptible – which includes his own personal sense of failure to save Tom and to imbue him with a rich, full life – into a figure of redemptive possibility, and to do so without losing sight of our capacity to wreak harm upon the lives of others, near or far. This, too, is a subject that Oliver's poetry cleaves to throughout his career.

Ian Brinton's selection makes available for the contemporary reader a wonderfully rich and representative array of Oliver's various modes and self-avowed responsibilities, from the domestically intimate, phenomenological prosody of his early poems, to the fully-fledged formalist adventures in dream-vision and burlesque satire of the 1980s and 1990s, to the anti-imperialist exhortations of *A Salvo for Africa* (2000). There are inevitably omissions in any edition of this sort. Readers wishing to fill in the gaps are directed in the first instance towards the initial collection of Oliver's poetry, the aptly titled *Kind* (London, Lewes, Berkeley: Allardyce, Barnett, 1987), still available from the publisher in the cloth-bound edition (<http://www.abar.net>), and which brings together Oliver's full (and variously revised) poetic output from 1969 to 1985, including *Oppo Hectic*, *In the Cave of Suiccession*, *The Diagram Poems*, *The Infant and the Pearl*, poems associated with *The Harmless Building*, and several uncollected poems. The full text of the otherwise out-of-print *Penniless Politics* is available via institutional or library access through the ProQuest Literature Online database. Oliver's posthumously published double-memoir-cum-biography of himself and the French revolutionary anarchist Louise Michel, *Whisper 'Louise'* (2005), is still available from the publisher, Reality Street (<http://www.realitystreet.co.uk>). There are a number of online resources that contain texts by Oliver, as well as scholarship, appreciation, and reminiscence of his life and work, of which especial mention should be made of the 'Douglas Oliver Hyper-Link Crystal', maintained by Edmund Hardy on the Intercapillary Space website (<http://intercapillaryspace.blogspot.com>). Scans of the complete runs of the magazines *Scarlet* (1990–1991) and *Gare du Nord* (1997–1999), which Oliver edited with the poet Alice Notley, his second wife, are available on Nick Sturm's website (<https://www.nicksturm.com>). Oliver's papers are held in the Albert Sloman Library at his *alma mater*, the University of Essex.

I would like to thank Dunstan Ward and Luke Roberts for their helpful comments on drafts of this preface.

JOE LUNA
Brighton, 2020

Introduction: 'infinity of the instant'

As if recognising a debt to a European cultural past, Douglas Oliver's Preface to the posthumously published Salt edition of *Arrondissements* immediately evokes an echo of Dante:

> More than mid-way through my life I have begun writing *Arrondissements*, a series of books or long sequences in poetry and prose, designed to reflect the world at large through the prism of Paris.

Three years later in August 2006 when Lee Harwood was being interviewed by Andy Brown for *The Argotist Online* he referred to a letter he had received from Oliver suggesting that 'Inside the harm is a clearing' and this is also an echo but this time of the American world of Herman Melville who wrote in *Moby Dick* about how when whales have young they form a circle of protection around them. Melville suggested that for some strange reason the water in that inner circle remains always very calm.

In 1973 Oliver's novel *The Harmless Building* was published jointly by Tim Longville's Grosseteste Review Books and Andrew Crozier's Ferry Press and this prose fiction was the first substantial piece of writing to appear after the death of his son Tom, who had been born with Down's syndrome in 1969. As John Hall was to point out in a review of later work this publication was 'the first to engage directly with the ideas of harm and harmlessness that Tom's life and death had prompted'. The absolute seriousness of Douglas Oliver's novel was evident from its opening statement:

> For the moment the truth is hiding in obstreperous fiction. I can, however, say that a real mongol baby died and that his memory affects my life.

With a humble and courteous disclaimer near the novel's opening Oliver tells the reader that 'my life is nothing special, no more exciting than average' but he then focuses our attention on the central question concerning our awareness of the immediate present:

> The project here will not be speed, poise, style, or the crossbow whizz of thought, though that may seem the project. Instead,

> I should love to keep a mongol baby alive in my mind, an outgoingness and kindness, a lack of coherence, an area of almost no-harm like a clearing in the middle of harm.

In a 'letter written to Douglas Oliver' by J.H. Prynne, published in 1973 in *Grosseteste Review 6*, we are given a moment of insight into the reactions of one intelligent reader and the insight radiates out from that point:

> Really I think this whole achievement is quite overwhelming. Attention worked out so closely does not often attain to a condition of truth. The trust usually asked of us is textual, or "human" like a friendly dog. But both together is so absolutely delicate and fine. I cannot say how deeply affected I am by having read this book.

Perhaps that 'outgoingness and kindness' is closely related to Douglas Oliver's focus upon the importance of the individual moment, an honest awareness of the present, and an understanding that the 'gravity of a poem lies in its whole form, and the prosody alone, being part of that unity, is sufficient access to it without the performer having to feel anything'. The tensions that rest between the creation of a poem and its source within the poet were noted by Oliver in an unpublished letter he wrote from Brightlingsea to Andrew Crozier in August 1974. Having just finished reading Crozier's long poem *Pleats* Oliver recognised that 'there has been a close relationship between the poetic consciousness and the *reported* event which has affected both sides of that tension in a way that I immediately recognise as profound'.

In an obituary of the poet written for *The Independent* in April 2000 Nicholas Johnson pointed to one of the central qualities of Douglas Oliver's poetry when he drew attention to the manner in which his writings 'investigated the instability of language, pitched against the language of political and social upheaval, grief and human vulnerability'. With this struggle for a language that can bring into focus both the world of socially political ideas and the personal anguish of an individual reality we might do well to turn back to that Lee Harwood interview in which he was asked 'Is there a home in the distant city or is the home here and now?' Harwood's answer was uncompromisingly clear:

> Well, my interpretation is that it's got to be the here-and-now, whether you like it or not! That's the real.

It is Douglas Oliver's engaged concern for the real that was made prominent by his friend Greg Chamberlain and published as a part of the *Guardian* obituary:

> Doug Oliver was never the kind of poet who shuts himself off from the world… He was game for just about anything – "Material!" he would say with a twinkle in his eye.

Oliver's Preface to *Arrondissements* brings to our attention that there are 'whole districts of my adopted city' which have 'dense concentrations of individual nationalities; to name them would be to name much of the world': Material!

Given this focused interest in the immediate it is not surprising that Douglas Oliver's poetry possesses an exactness of detailed understanding that should bring to mind the lines from George Oppen's 'The Men of Sheepshead' (*The Materials*, 1962) in which the American poet brought into focus the men who worked in a town at the south end of Brooklyn. Oppen spoke of 'material', of things:

> End-for-end, butted to each other,
> Dove-tailed, tenoned, doweled – Who is not at home
> Among these men? who make a home
> Of half-truth, rules of thumb
> Of cam and lever and whose docks and piers
> Extend into the sea so self-contained.

And it is exactly that precision of engagement with reality that Oliver recognised as central when he wrote about the art of writing poems in his review of John James's *The Small Henderson Room* published in *Cambridge News* in 1969:

> We know most surely what a man is not from the immediate content of his words, but from the way he approaches us in the conversation, and how this expresses the deeper content of what he is saying.

Twenty-five years later, in an essay on 'Poetry's Subject' written for *PN Review* (September-October 1995) Douglas Oliver was to bring his focus sharply to bear upon the importance of being a poet by stating in unequivocal terms that ' A poet's full performance is the whole life's work; and it is for that he or she finally takes responsibility'. He went on to say, in terms that resonate strongly as we look at his oeuvre, that after the poet's death 'individual poems will be seen as part of that overall project, even if they didn't seem so at the time'.

With its close understanding of how the form and presentation of poetry is inextricably bound up with an awareness of the compassionate nature of an 'outgoingness and kindness', defining itself as a 'clearing in the middle of harm', it is important for us to return to that section of *Three Variations on the Theme of Harm* (Paladin Poetry, 1990) where a prose piece precedes the short poem 'For Kind':

> The whole form lies in the 'unconscious' of the poem; it is its ineffable nature, just as I have a nature developed in me by birth and upbringing. Even if, as I was, we're brought up in some middle-class, snobbish, racist suburb, once we touch more profoundly natural unconscious sides of ourselves all the cultural rubbish falls away and we recognize a deep kinship, an international kinship.

An overwhelming sense of honesty threads its path through these poems and as he put it in 'For Kind':

> Kindness acts idly or unnaturally,
> leads you into fear. Act in kind.
> Kindness makes you idle, worse, unnatural.
> Don't be afraid of the darkness of kind.

It was perhaps no haphazard decision of Anthony Barnett's that his 1987 Allardyce, Barnett publication of Douglas Oliver's work should be given the title *Kind* just as it was entirely appropriate that a comment from Patrick Wright writing in *London Review of Books* should appear on the back cover of that volume:

> Grounded in personal experience, the writing nevertheless has the literary capacity to transform everything it finds there…

It is also of immense importance that Oliver's epigraph placed at the opening of the first collected poems should simply point out

Always for Tom

Oppo Hectic

For Jan

When I Was in Bridport

You know I'm working Jan, you know
I am John. From up here your chairs
scrape oceanically all the time and
birds shriek, sheafs
of first drafts wing from my desk.
These wills I'm writing, don't think of
floating paper darts from a
cliff-face. It can't be
morning though shadows slant that
way and the sea's a blue flat, not
struggling over much sand. The air's
not crystal but orange against
a sandstone fortress
pitted with flaws and it holds an imprisoned
population. My childhood
of a static shoreline: I
craned upwards towards
the dark prison holes where birdmen
sent out gulls thrown
in a flight-line along the face, bruised wing-tips.
I thought then that quality was in
the hardly-seen arm-movements, the wind after
taking a white scrap in its direction, that
others might throw stones to disappear in the sea.
That beach, archæologically, was
prehistoric. So much
of cliff-flights are layers below
the level of the present-day town.
                                    This
is not a plea for more industry, or you could
joke about flights above the town, how there's
always the aeroplane. I'm just precise
about the level I start from.
To go below it is a final prison, a kind of burial.

The earthen stairs

The smallest news I have of you is rays of
spore, a black sun we stand on. What I hear
of you is where we meet. Draw
the centre blackness up round
us. Earth's surface is above. At
the top of some stairs each step the
barrier goes down. We fall about. Down.
You're old-fashioned enough to take
my hand slung low at the level
of genitals. The moment we will speak has
already happened: it waits
in the silence in the subterranean hall
as meaning stumbles downstairs towards articulation.
Waiting too is an anxious group of friends. They
live in the news which we gingerly
tread. Our descent will reach
a cry deep in earth that unfreezes
roots in the blackness over our heads.
That's the yell of recognition, claspings
in the low hall when we join
these sharers of small news. May they renew
themselves where fresh spore
grows in the infertile levels. Stairs
have always led to this point but
we lost the way. I had to get
information from a medical specialist.

The Furnaces

                              Weak flame zone
still it's soon flame on a gas stove down the city's very
      end a weak resort of the pipe network. Lead tube
            extending forward has
                  a house on its tip
and spits light into a dark kitchen. In the tile surround
                              alternative gold circlets
spin. The enclosed cooker harbour burns with gas across water beneath
      a wide beach, as yet unpopulated. At
            its extremities an old port
            and the so-called new,
'new' because burning waves make ruins flicker on the sea bottom. So the flame
                              hovering on an invisible
moment of change is the least solitary fact of miles of gas
      sent to houses, waves of heat rolling
            under the tarmac and here
                  there are three towns:
the apparent is built on another—the one below uninhabitable
                              owing to corrupt air
the third is still tawny striations in gas vapour from the
      ground, its children having golden hair
            and clothes of gypsy yellow
                  materialising
at the gas flare's fiercest point; the invisible distance, before
                              such colours, remakes
time in its tremulous millimetres and this middle town
      is being remade in sulphur, leaden pipes
            melt underneath and we are no
                  longer masters
even of the miniature furnace on a hairbrained linotype machine.
                        Lead solidifies
into words, apt to quarrel, of all others fit to be assassins. And each
      house is remade a furnace too   the lights go on
            anxiety gives me again that old heart-
                  burn. Leonine children
are in the attic of a house ageing downwards to volatile corruption.

Oppo Hectic

There were father poets who spoke
with their mouths round an orange. Round with
the saucepan their beautiful eyes smoked their
dauphin's hair where the salt smoked
and so did Orpheus. Too much rope for the round
of the hat opening, a rind on an eagle's cunt, and the women
whose gloves gleamed, and the bushbaby, since he was early
for the poor guys, did not repeat the smoking of his ancestors.
It was far too easy. Or alternatively it was far too hard. Or
the seven pylons the women of course without the chicken-ridden
vegetables and their poetry books said Aaah Ooooh you've shit
Pushkin down the drain—incidentally why is no-one
necking near the drainaway? Looking at that grimace you wrote
a few words in excellent French, "the English scum
made it with their limbs." Like love-
rape the spirit of the gaoler fixes up a tight circus and
the alphabetical posture of the emprisioned men said where are
the poets who speak with their mouths round an orange? Their foe
rescues them: the ORANGES are really child-poets.

                                        (After Blaise Cendrars)

Ordnance Survey Map 178

I have never been to Woolland, downhill from
Long Wood, the park on our right until Skinner's farm
at the corner. My hands turn you
across the road, we don't take the left fork, it
peters out. The manor house is grey cardigan and needs
unbuttoning. This brussels sprout field is disordered
as we enter, blackbirds disappear
into the leaves and tick about electric
as brain impulses. I've seen too many churches,
enough like that one over the field, so Victorian
and weakened with green light. We define objects
first by symbols, eventually by movements away
from them, as black sparks scud at low level. Not
the steep hill, at least one in seven, up to Bulbarrow.
For each of us a body we now lay down. There's the deepest
green I've known in the sprout foliage cluttering our
heads. Among roots we are disturbed, aroused
by the intelligence of plants. Earth blotches our cheeks,
moulds to finger bones and rises over them. We struggle
on the floor of growth, under the stench of a deciduous
sky. After a while your head between
my palms lolls short-circuited. Your own
loose grip has filled with etheric water, icy rain spots
our clothes. Soaked, filthy, bursting
upright, transitional, we, the black earth fountaining,
detach ourselves from a lost field on the map. Join me
on the road going out; glance back if you like
Lot's wife, at a family behind us walking towards
Woolland, the parents of an old schoolfriend,
or maybe my parents. The brussels sprouts were
not possible, no-one I've met has ever been to
Woolland. I'll check
the rest of these facts tomorrow.

All those factories with offices in the roof girders

Dinosaur dung under the tail came hard
phosphatic nodules from that marble factory its dim
brain 12ft above ground. An authoress
nearby does kids' books with a dinosaur hero. Desmond. Althea Braithwaite.
My own kid calls coprolite nodules non-jewels. I've some still
in the car dashboard. They are fossil warts I say to
passengers and two I gave to the Folk Museum
who were short. It's lime phosphate, a fertiliser
prized by the Victorians. I can't
pledge it was actually dinosaurs, let's think
of them though: work to the 1850s with high wages, a neologism for
     my kid, a
publishing enterprise and who, extinct, weave their heads
above our affairs higher than ever could, say, beavers.

Mongol in the woods

(for Tom)

My son's eyes plead for expense I should otherwise
withhold. You're around. I might as well
pay it for you, not to some future man, Testicles,
when the balls descend, but to the unheroic maker
in him. May I use the word imbecile? We're in woods
where no-one can tell me not to. And
if we don't laugh brutally at the mongol's swollen tongue
that's as if everyone were no longer
mysterious. I think of more drawn
into his iris than just vacancy
decorated with a gelid ruff.
                                      Get out of this trance,
the internal restraints on muscle, the hooks in the
oily tissue. If we could only
stop his iris contracting in sunlight
we'd move. Never mind. Pick up
all the money standing in the woods and you
take it as if a gift sealing the voodoo. The pretence
opens his lips; some ectoplasm comes out
which doesn't belong to our thinking. He won't
be cured. Besides it's too much like
the food he's eaten. So my
word, love, attaches to the lining of
his oyster mouth; we'll let him
prosper it. Then Tom
will announce, one day: "My father's dead. You're my father."
That's why I'm confident my rebirth lies in his
right to deep feelings. Ours, though, are deeper.
It's a difference in skies because clouds never
change in his pupils and, once out of shade, on hot roads,
he crawls like an animal.

How long anything lasts

I

Old teeth are to taint the vowels
adopt word-craft
               of Victorian yokels
syllables to
grow tufts of hair and I'm conscious
of this death 1886 William Barnes
he dressed differently conscious of his
life   cassock knee-length trousers   buckled shoes
thrown by a chair   blankets up
to the prophet head.   Between us
not 80 years   some
other kind of time-lag
               memory
can't hold on to
hesitates in the rectory bedroom
a stone face locates a
smile that dies
pillow flowing with white hair.

II

Slates   will move   over thatch
then themselves dislodge.
My eyes that night has overtaken see his
faith a ram-
        shackle house
the place shuts in
             a piece of childhood marred
             a dog's hollow bark
             to menace the threshold.

I forget how / long anything lasts
the late bus
missed so waiting by the locked
door one message to try this house with   please
switch on your light
                       hope is
no more than a surprise movement of the
gullet if my throat's closed.

Steadily behind this door
people are going to
bed ending last century
listen for the
demolition the
house not weather sound   rainy
eaves that harbour the parson's voice
                                budge
                                unfit
already the staircase
gone but uncannily years slipper up past
the stair window
candles borne against
freckled glass / goes black
shadows in the bedroom
coverlets move over the white hair till there's
only a smooth bed.

The Context of the War

(for Bob Peters)

Polished shoes above black acrylic; that's right
in context. Such as a chapel of rest. I'm warring
against what seems right at the time.
Insects crawl at height in my hair, even the dimmed
light here can attract them – only good for one
day, feet-suckers clogged with virus. I can't criticise
the people running this ceremony, for I'm too quiet-toned
and they unsuspectingly observe the bereaved whose em-
otions are to be costly. Fine if they'd be tight-fisted
against soft palms; all the same I'll soon lie
on the broad-clothed back of the funeral director while
women pay their bills. They also pay for me
for insects, polished shoes, and a place
to leave relatives. There's still
the caskets black and shiny and
the first one I look into is a child's. That is the
context of the war. Not fought. Small feet
in circuits outside mine. Not fought this quietly.

The Diagram Poems

for Ted Berrigan and Alice Notley

The diagrams plot and transform movements of several groups of raiders as they make commando-style seizures of key sites in a single town and eventually try to escape.

For example, the first diagram is of a general co-ordinator's movements as he visits the various operations by car.

In the second diagram, one group of raiders, some disguised as airmen, arrives in three separate parties to take over a police station. (Beforehand, they have reconnoitred the station during several visits, posing as members of the public. They brought the same dog, twice, for vaccination formalities.) They begin the seizure by rounding up policemen and placing them, eventually, in cells. A police sergeant, overlooked, appears from a dormitory, fires warning shots to the outside streets, darts through corridors, and aims at the invaders from a central patio. He takes refuge, wounded, in the dormitory and finally gives himself up. Two other police officers walk into the building and are overpowered but a third escapes. These prove crucial hitches in the over-all plan.

The other diagrams describe taking over a fire station and the central telephone exchange, raids on three banks, and the final getaway.

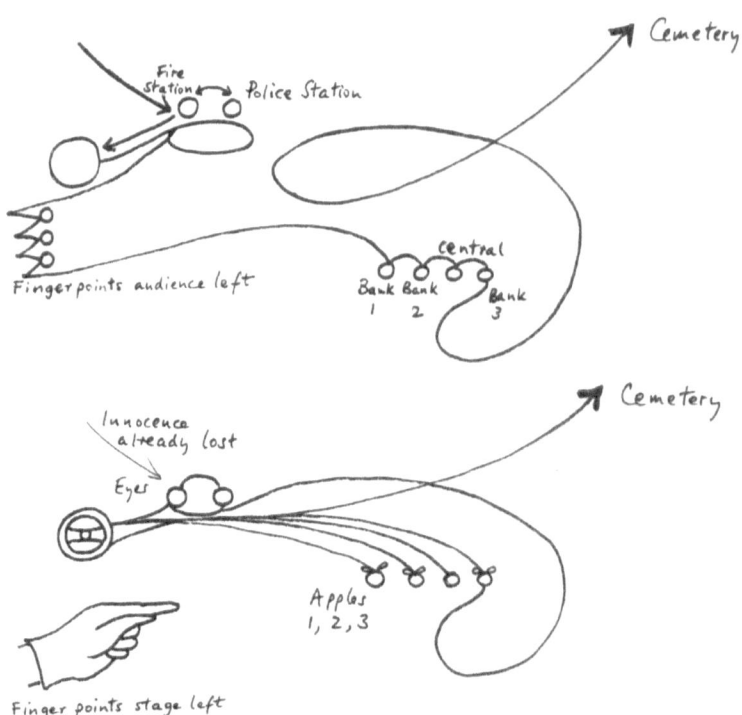

Team Leader

He switches on internal driver
his gloves mirror an inset which is
a steering wheel from side to side
blood will hurry past everyone onlooking
the tasselled finger points left
but final direction rests up the team sleeves
into the cemetery there.

Already bereaved of innocence and late, he
hops along to two spectacle lenses
finds that eyes are sighting along gun arms
waits for a white handkerchief to wave
and with relief
nips back to tell people I can't name
that looped progress to the apples should begin
without snags or
bends a correct slither.
Visits the eyes bowls number of miles
before the teams gather at the crook of elbow
in the hollow where car axles break
and the thing carries off awkwardly, with losses.

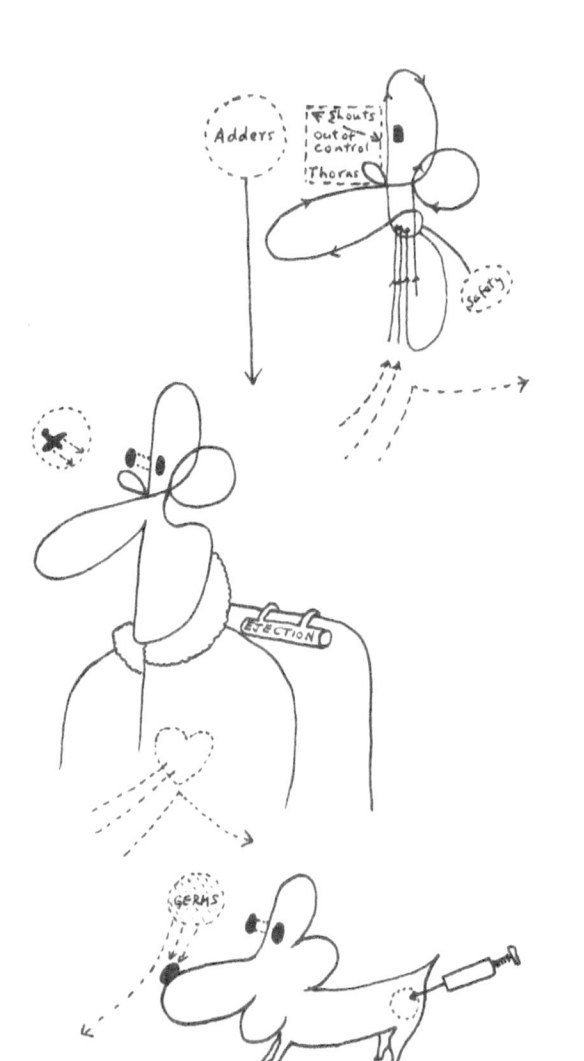

P.C.

Blue conjurors in corridors
hope to go straight and quick
immobilise a commissariat and –
grab him, no curving into turbulence –
Sergeant My Namesake bursts
from arcanum into hostile communication
shoots twice, breaking glass,
misfires in the overgrown patio.
That grass is all warning shouts.
We've already had delays of team leader
now loud white thorns
grow in the plans.
Like an adder, the sergeant
swerves to cold. From a doorsill he snakes
into the internal.
The hope of speed is stung in a home of pyjamas
or a bullet to the fancy for a long, long time.
At last, in a dreamy sweat, movement
goes peaceably to the sagpit, safety.

An English voice sneaks to the ear,
interfering, across time,
we are your servants can we help you
to the most dangerous daisy love of sleep?
Such sleep hangs in the parachute
dynamic of an old-fashioned aviator
ejecting from arrowed lines;
his sinker heart houses concubine pistols
which shoot him up internally
in the incurable warfare of the adult
and the intercom's alive with ancient panic

or, another inset, sleep is
droopy with a half-disease

like a vaccinated dog
pulsy as lame
Mount Pleasant piss-off breed.

All foreigners to these three visions
come to their portals to surrender
except, importantly, just one who is fearful
and hurries away before entering
so none of the other movements can be complete.

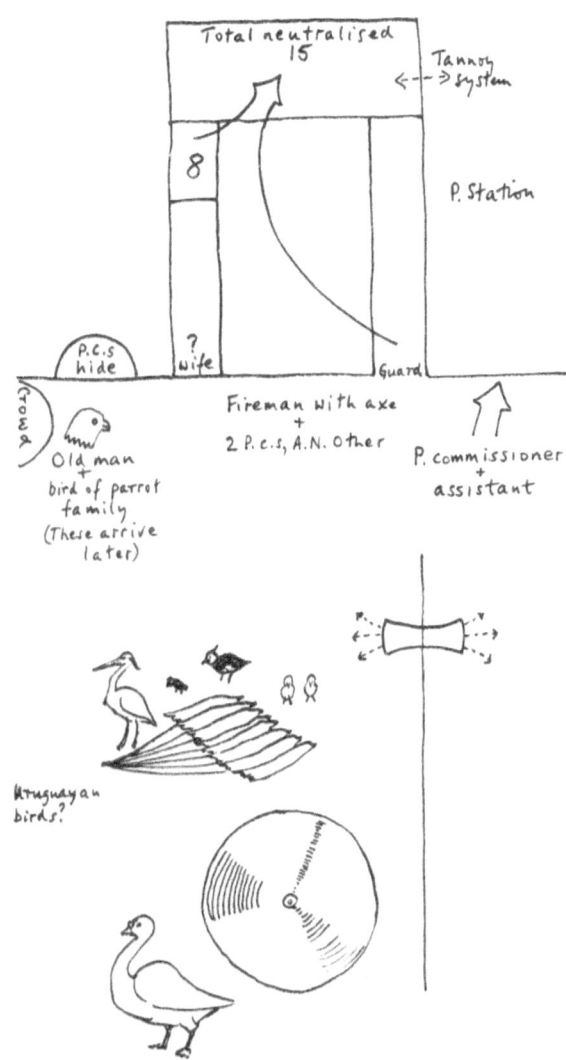

The Fire Station

Ill wings tied down: the birds would sing
a different story from the one we're in,
an old story of firemen's bravery.
It's cast in an unwelcome, mocking light
just because unsuited to these escapades,
as our great tale chimes on the air
misrepresents the fire axis, turns it
into a clarion tannoy.
These firebirds had been notably dozy
and easily caught, and yet for the teams
a captured axe becomes totemic
in the year of risk of lives
men and women, women and men there now
but some in appalling prisons. Why do I
allow this publicity?
It's my wish to make public the blank of the eye
which may be full of real fire demons,
not these dozers. It's something in my eye
has rung the bland alarm bell.
It shouldn't ring, the birds
would have stayed tied down
starting no other species off clucking.

Not yet in the picture, an old man to come
to leave mystery boxes in the midst of our axis.
A parrot, essence of cremation colours,
whose parent is cinders and whose sons fly red,
this demon parrot, not yet in the picture,
will shoulder his way out of the boxes
tongue scolder screeching alarms louder
than scratchy tannoys
to annoy certain forces of danger
that run in but, alarmed, pull up short;
this demon, I say, will announce
the ignored years between us and the fire station
at grand cries.

Central

I heard and slowly understood but then I saw
and I saw years ahead in the light of the eye centre
as I'd dimly heard years past in the sound of the earpiece.
I saw our ageing and I could get it. I saw the airman signal
and I got it. I heard Tom's voice as from a distant receiver
and I got it. Seven guerrillas tying up the telephone exchange
expertly. Then Tom's voice said, "Hallo Central",
from the booth of death.

In the first days of jellyroll, Tom was my son.
Tom, go ahead.
"Ring my mother; it's an emergency. She's with child
again, by herself. Ring her."
I'll get us some eye medicine.
"No. Ring. In a couple of minutes we sever
our links. The guerrillas have
cut the cables. Condition major immediate…
it's the end of the line and here's a…"
(Still Tom's voice, the past ahead of me, but fading. I'd
better put that down to feeling and feeling's
part of my work.) "Yes, it is part…Don't put down
the receiver…" (fading) "…the ear hears with feeling…"
(fading, cut dead).

They'd already neutralised *le standard* by standard procedures
Oh Tom, go ahead.
neutralised the risk by risk, though some raiders will die
Tom, go ahead.
and I'd like to have friends on these streets, friends
who'd look for me in creations of total emergency
in or out of dreams… Cut… A guerrilla command tone:
"Place the pregnant
woman into the temporary prison with the 40

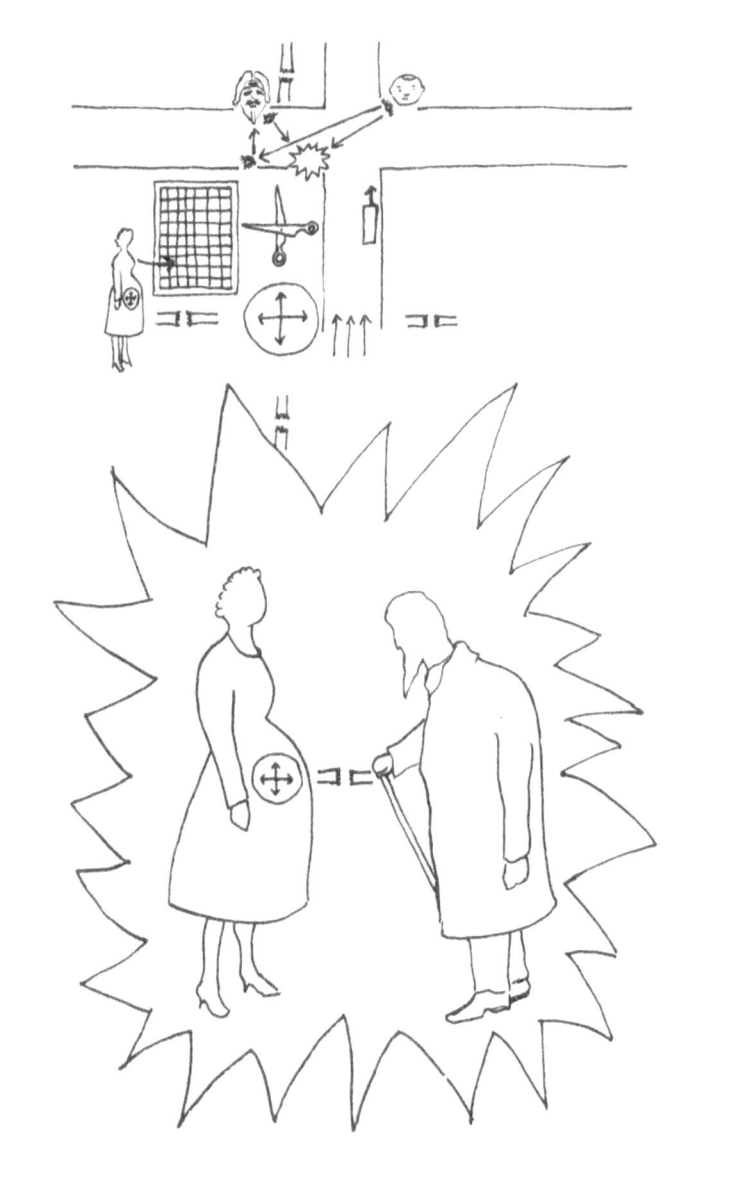

communication functionaries and consumers. Get on with this.
Cut other connections yourself but obey
the voices that come from long distance, obey sound and feeling."

Tom, go ahead.
But my Tom's in a frightener cell
of the night of youth
where old and young eyes shine and are grey
and the ears fold in
to the internal sounds.

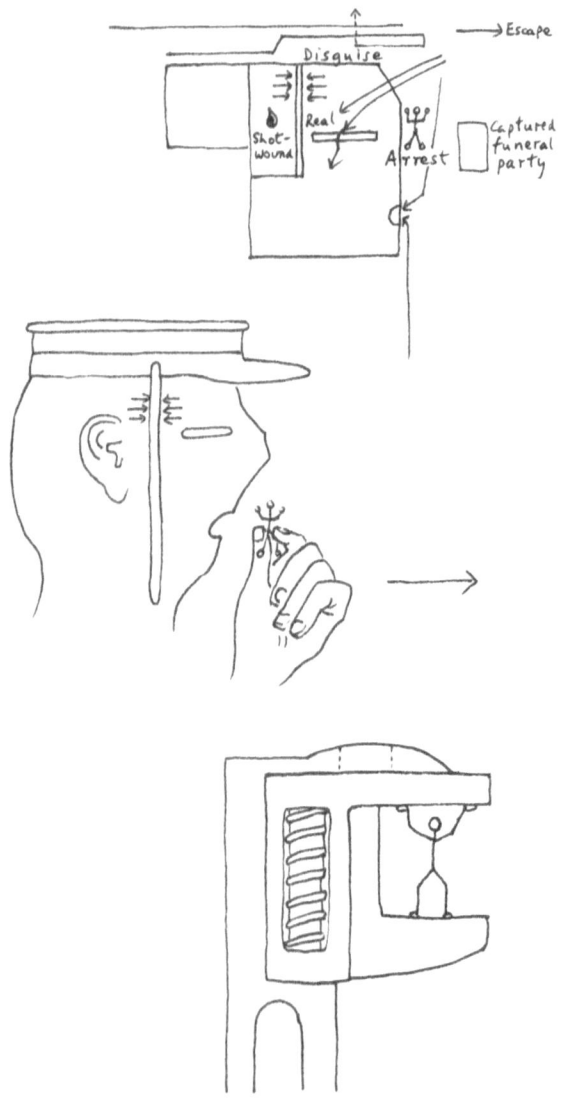

Arrest

…Lunchtime over, manager not in his hidey hole
but he is in his cubby hole with those who hope to be managers too.
And here's a real P.C. confronting a false P.C. and giving in.
No money will be drawn from the bank this lunchtime
except all of it
that's why you'll not find any drawn in the diagram
except all of it
which is invisible to anyone who doesn't think
the whole is its parts; that is, visible to the rapacious
who like real heads on their coins
I mean, of flesh,
which you can't use for bulk purchase
though a flesh wound is the price
for this bulk withdrawal by bank robbers
while on the pavement the disguised P.C.
looks a bit like "Serving Us", the many-headed dog.

The shot! as I imply; and it affects hearing so totally
we wait in vain for voices once again to float in across time,
like Tom's.
Damaged in the ear so badly that we fail to hear sufficiently
of the true loss from the office wound:
the gone sick, the suicidal deafness, and, finally,
the arrest when the heart's no longer heard in the ear,
even if the heart-beat still receives its "bravos!" from the crowd,
but also suffers from betrayal (by the crowd?)
and the part gets captured by the whole –
if that is a whole which makes the span of life
so inevitable and yet adjustable.

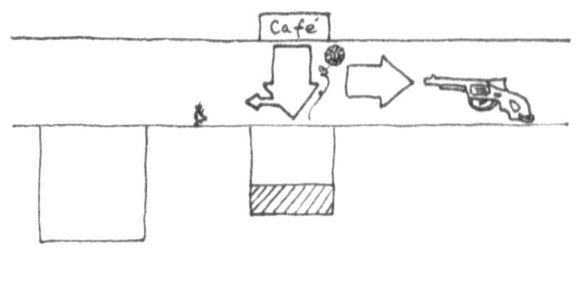
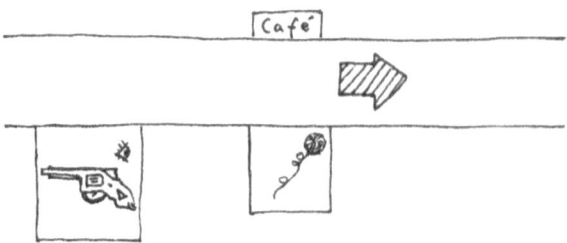

Gold

Here's the mid-point of this fortune; we hit the phenomenon
of almost-zero snag: between two hazardous
and likely banks of dread here a small bank
where money, a peaceable liquid,
can be siphoned off; it only needs time.
And that's what we start with just when it all felt
jumpy. It's a clear path
across the street from the café to the bank
straight through the heart of mid-loathing.
One possible giveaway, an observer eye, is whisked off
to another bag of troubles altogether; in fact
to the next bank of troubles, money as magnet,
diagram unlucky seven.
In this mid-point, the cause is hurried, but bothered
by little more than a mother with her child;
they're soft as wool, but unfortunately they must go
into temporary stir. Oh if only all went
like this, with a P.C.'s gun snout merely trembling
in the acquiescence from fear and is that acquiescence?
Well, that's an old question, when I can't even know
whether to leave the coffers so light
cures a single… I must not ask that question here, no right;
let's say gold in physic is a cordial and the gilt
liquid is taken off; then escape if you can
into the arrow of time replete with gold
and directed futurewards by a will
that isn't mine, this arrow stuttering on
as the teams grow
ever richer in goods, information, but not luck.

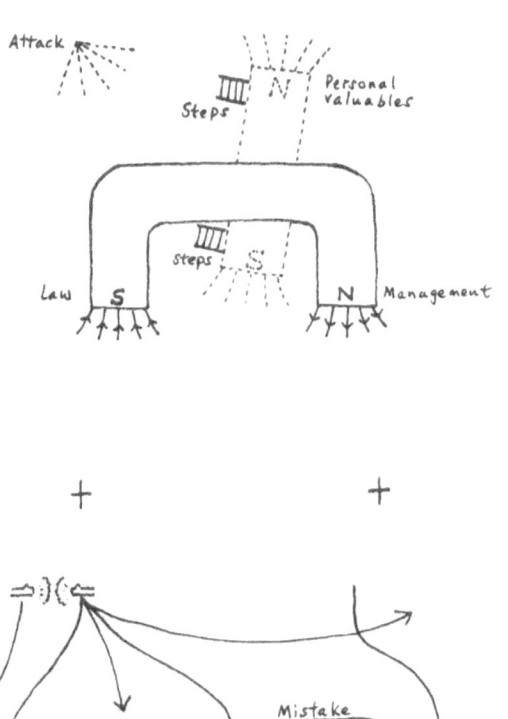

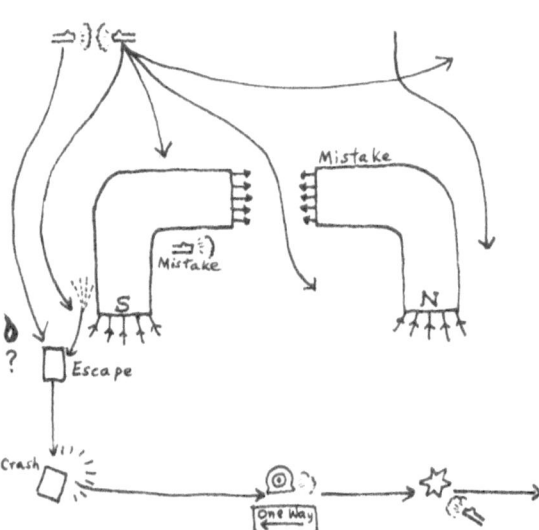

U

The lost child's voice breaks in my throat: no time
for it, softness unheard, a gurgle as a third bank's doors
open quietly to receive attackers. Once more
the set up, the planted "customers" at the retreating U
of a magnetic counter. Now, my children,
in the warning world, lying abroad
or playing with a magnet theatre here at home,
now the forces of life are few and precious and this magnetism is one
commandeered by the banking magnates, by the magnet of their will,
pulling at money through their management and managers
in the hierarchies of their laws. They invest
their fields of force with the hardest law of all:
no casualties above the ground: all hoarding likewise
underground. This is the law which sends
directions through the silver, turns it base,
and binds it to the secret selves
which, deep below, increase in value like jewels.

The lost child's voice should speak softly but undyingly
across a land silvery with democracy
and glistening with wheat, trembling at the spoken kindness;
the voice should temper the muttering
of bank clerks across the mica counters
and ring in the money slipping from their fingers.
We know this. Everyone. But we let the voice break in our throats
the laughs, little distinguished from coughs,
echo discreetly across stone floors;
softness unheard;
until a man with a light machine gun this day
springs on to the cash desk and, astride there,
we know this, waves the muzzle where all the arrows
of acquisition, law and management have come and gone.

We know Tom's voice, we now know this, we see
the magnets sunder in half, induced repulsion
in every sense of order, and soon, my children
in the warned world, the street awakes to shots
and enemies and wounds and chivalries
and carelessness and showdowns, and innocent bystanders
left to bleed behind an arrow pointing to an unseen cemetery.
The voice breaks unheard across a land formerly silvery
but changed to iron law and deep repulsion.
Yes, there was an attack; it cut the magnet's U in half,
I don't need to tell you but I do, softly,
that I am my children;
in me their voice breaks with the ear knowledge.

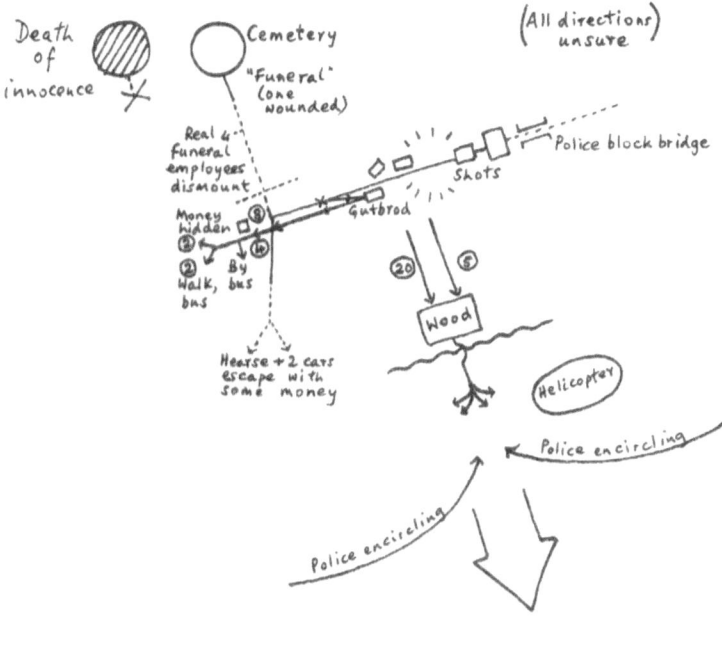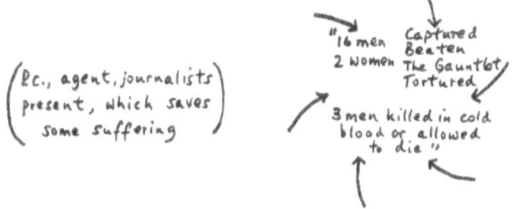

The Diagonal Is Diagonal

Slowness of gaze, the slowness behind fear
perception
calm thoughts staying in the mist
above a waterfall from the left: but what of the speed
of calmness, since it doesn't stay still?
The wavering of lights doesn't
but moves in remote consequence to
foam at its fastest.
Compare sudden crying to the slowness of this funeral
but it's a fake and speeds up
compare that to the speed of capture
to the rush of a diagonal
the arrow of a bad thought pell-mell towards torture
the pool of suffering arrowed in
and the calm grace of courage that coexists
with those speeds and with the sick other face of slowness.
I do not name the incidents
lest I should seem to lay claim to them,
but I little own this poem; it is nothing
without the original movements.
The diagram could again spring a picture
encircling looks like buttocks,
there's a cloaca. Wolves.
But I should say hardly anything else about that,
my right is minimal.
I let a Parisian journalist in me draw the pictures
let him have his head
it was an academic drew the arrows and the loss of hope
letting him
but now the picture transforms no longer; it is the picture.
The place of reassembly in the cemetery
really is the cemetery
prepared for the ashes of human conduct
and the fires of human behaviour so rotten in origin

that animals whose dead are not cremated
have knowledges above the festival here
and every nerve's alive in me
down the swift diagonal
that slants from the cemetery in courage
and takes the poem almost entirely from me.
Almost in humility and loathing I kneel
at the feet of the next account
which is of bestiality and sadism
so mucky it makes the scalp creep.
It is my dead son who always brings me to this point
of innocence in the heart of swift cruelty
and speed of pictorial change won't get to it
and the poetry won't move from it
that innocent point exactly neighbour to that other start
from which team leader became a finger pointing left,
that's audience left: for the teams
the old sinister direction was, from the beginning,
the cemetery. In the known risk then
an airman became a dog
firemen were pegged down as birds of fire
the baby in the womb was old
the pinman strained against the spanner
if you could only believe he'd hold that posture
an arrow filled with gold
the magnet power of money failed
as a magnet power of luck did
as the magnet power of self-control
as a magnet power of being funny
in situations which don't call for wit to *be* funny
all these started in the drawings from the point
neighbour to
the point at which the innocence stays clean
the diagonal does not speed down
to these loaded reversals
police exchange no shots
there's no sequel of bestiality.

And yet we're carried downwards by a foreign courage here
that we have no right to justify
(lest innocence should run that gauntlet too)
no right to borrow it, jig it into shapes,
display it like a wound on our own opening palm.
But, lacking the one innocence, we are driven into this foreign time
into falseness in funerals, rehearsals
leading from the cemetery;
it all turns so really funereal for us
as brave as that and as flawed
just a final diagram almost straight
and a heart on which the diagram is scored
beside the deaths of innocences we have known
and even caused a little in the scarface heart.
We cannot ask the prisoners to forgive
our foreign nations
but we may hope the dead can kiss
for us the face of innocence in the rushing dark
and grace and courage arrive calmly in us.

The Infant and the Pearl

I

Lying down in my father's grey dressing gown
its red cuffs over my eyes, I caught sight
of Rosine, my pearl, passing out of my room
one night while a dream passed out of the night
of my nation. What a robe she was wearing! Brown
and sinewy, lion colours in the doorlight;
she turned, Laura-like, on her face a light frown
to be leaving, not reproving but right-
lipped, reddish hair loving the dead
facial centre: virtue could've kept her
had I enough of it, though I dreamt of it.
In my grey gown I would have gladly slept by her.

I was wrangling in my grey gown, full of wrath
as the door closed. And I felt close to me
the paternal cloth quietening, the rough
flannel lie flat in darkness; if even the
diagonal doorlight had been cut off
in the night of my nation, if even the
much-hoped-for Rosine had just had enough
of the dream – a fragment of light finally
dying in the room – well, the realm in my
closed eyes came alive with one colour:
the rosy-red pearl, so rich and womanly.
I shuddered in the grey for I should have slept by her.

Pearl, whose rose grey gleams
with infant hints in the hinterland
of my dreams, as when any poet dreams
of a lost pearl – some principle refound
only by resting on a gravestone! Rosine's
the mother of policy, priced beyond
our suspect neo-patriotism. She seems
in my nights to radiate reddish beams
as if whatever our actions she gladdened

our unseen selves, while without her our
conscious selves are immeasurably saddened.
In my grey gown I would have gladly slept with her.

The self that shines in the greying sunshine
of the immediate is actual, though it is
not all that is there. The feminine
is numinous in my masculine: it isn't nonsense
to picture a pearl placed on a shrine
inside myself; on the swirling surface
is Rosine's reflection which, as if she's been crying,
half turns away, ashamed where her mercy's
judged socialistic, too soft for justice.
For the dream isn't Margaret; the pearl's true minister
would be as lustrous as Rosine is…
In my grey gown I would have gladly slept with her.

My thinking greyed; the vision eventually
flickered in half-sleep – then Rosine had fled,
a fastidious foe of the tin pan alley
serious, powdered, severed head
of Margaret, whose self serially
repeated, televised, pearlized, and reported
ten times, tampered with immediacy.
An empty voice in my empty head…
and sexual absence inhabiting my bed…
like a vacuum in a vacuum, except for the
cuffs on my eyes, recall of red…
I shuddered in the grey for I should have slept with her.

II

A grey light dawned and on the distant
hills that I dreamt of lay a city of disdain
circled with steel walls, with silent
spires like warheads, in which one pane

gleamed in bleak agate; an arrogant
city above countryside that a murrain
seemed to have hit: a hoar-frost-land,
medieval, the poor and the mighty again
in the chivalric hierarchy, but no golden chain
of charity joining them, just the martinet
reign of chance ruling commerce, in whose train
come prosperity, perils and probably regret.

The hills, though, were free, free of disorder,
hills of privilege, of prerogative governance,
a régime arising from the ruins of order:
lording it over the lean shires, once
the same Britain, now they were Britain's border,
an encircling supreme around happenstance.
And I was a new-style, a knowing dreamer,
though a grey friar flying over foetid expanse,
whose unfortunate fields were unfertilized by Providence;
where medieval was modern and where Margaret
ruled without Rosine, true mercy, while Chance
bred possible prosperity, perils, or regret.

In this landscape of chance, all at once a Churchillian
ghosting of blue graced the hills' far clothing,
yet the soil near at hand rotted, and the sillion
reeked. Brother ploughman ploughed with loathing,
knowing some were making a million
out of the serving classes and saving
their compassion like credit, crowing at each minion
the slogan, 'Supply and Demand,' mouthing
the language of natural law, laughing
off as nonsense that 'natural', though Margaret
legislates, is Chance, and legalizes nothing
but possible perils or probable regret.

In my dream I dreaded those hills, for they meant
a journey through ruins to a winter horizon.

Two whole epochs half merged, a convent
looked like a failed factory, the device on
its gate a graffito against unemployment,
as if nuns would denounce anyone who relies on
the medium, money, to act as agent
of *arete*, allowing self-love to alight on
the back of social like a lion with flies on
intent to rape. The resolve of Margaret
is rare, but lets flies randomize on
Britain's prosperity, bringing perils or regret.

The hills receded as I ran to them through
a badly-enervated wood, environmentally
ill, i.e., thin trees were into so-so
leaning away from each other. And the lichen
was the same as my flaking psoriasis – so
the dry edge of my heart had evidently
infected both flora and my face with psycho-
somatic, fallacious sickness. Silently,
across a noisome stream, a blue Bentley
awaited me. I could tell that Margaret
might be in it by its pennant. It was empty, but apparently
proffered prosperity, perils or regret.

III

In such dreams the river kills time, and regret
faces those who fearlessly dive in:
they don't drown like Leander but like the Pearl Poet
awake no hero, having hoped for a life in
Eternity. There was *timor mortis* in this rivulet,
green as grimy greenbacks and striving in
vain to meander. Though I didn't forget
that time is money, the time half alive in
all currency couldn't thrive in the current. 'To connive in
cutting down cash flow,' I reasoned, 'takes vision.'

And the Bentley had a beckoning glove in
a doorlight grainy blue-grey like television.

If the stream smelt stagnant, the blue saloon
had tyres whose walls would keep white for ever.
But shouldn't I stay safely on my own
side, pure because purposeless? For wherever
the Bentley was bound, I was bound pretty soon
to ride out of reality altogether,
like a puerile *Private Eye* lampoon.
The car's petrol compartment cover
flipped open on the flank. That 'come hither'
glove waved in the window with derision.
From the front emerged a gnomic chauffeur,
his livery grainy blue-grey like television.

The chauffeur's blue suit was of airy weave,
a half transparent screen through which the trees
ghosted. We might honour Airey Neave,
but this was more Saatchi (or Saatchi), who said, 'Please
come over to us, Sir; it's a short step. We've
a special personage waiting and she's
both your will and your way.' Flashing his teeth,
he unlatched the rear door and I crossed dead leaves
to join him, jumping the current, ill at ease
to enter this Bentley – a betrayal of socialism.
There was still no-one inside, simply voices
in a light grainy blue-grey like television.

'Are you blue spirits spirits of Tories?'
I asked as I whoofed into an English hide
seat. 'I thought these Bentleys had lavatories,'
I joked as the voices whirled confusedly. A wide
arm rest fell down for me and my worries
dulled over. The foul air outside
was, inside, as fragrant as fairy stories
and the chauffeur was bending down beside

my door, fuelling the car with Countryside
Stagdeflation Mixture from the stream. My decision
as we started was a gentlemanly raid
on a drinks tray in the blue-grey like television.

Why the air was so blue Christ knows!
I wasn't swearing, wasn't sipping 'Cure us, Howe',
that blue liqueur once imbibed by bibulous
bankers; but the gin glowed blue and through
the air curled blue billows
of writhing, polaroid shapes; a shadow,
a scent, beside me. 'She comes and goes
like this,' crackled the chauffeur. 'The video
reception in here hasn't been how
we like it.' 'You mean my imagination
is persuaded,' I said, 'that our premier's now
just a grainy blue-grey like television?'

IV

The blue bonnet with its proud little 'B'
for Bentley or Britain coasted like a boat
under the barren boughs. 'Hitachi
have fiddled with logic control and come out
with what you'd anticipate, adjustable futurity,'
chuckled my driver. 'It's the actual's antidote,
the future replayed in the present, jitter-free:
a revision of what hasn't happened. What
we do is this: we project into spot
x, say your dream, a futurity reader
function that monitors the future mote
in your eye and the beam in the eye of our leader,

and replays a replica leader onto the screen
of the present, holographically if we have
to.' (In the front passenger seat came the sheen

of a thin, televisual figure, a grave,
black-coated man assembling.) 'Do you mean,'
I replied, 'it's really her replica? What of
the actual Mrs Thatcher?' 'Actual, in a dream?
Have you taken leave of your senses? We save
the actual for believers. You'll have to behave
as if all responses are real.' 'But we need a
true guide to the future, not a TV wraith.'
'In *your* eye – not in the eye of our leader.'

The leader herself 'switched on' – I suppose
you'd say – beside me, though with some 'tearing'
of her upper torso towards me, the nose
angled aggressively, though the whole was caring
in demeanour despite being dislocated. I froze
in panic at such a celebrity. She was wearing
a pearly suit, not silver-rose
pink, since sadly we seemed to be sharing
a black, blue and white world. But the bearing
of the front passenger meant a man for the media
to deal with delicately: a Joseph for dreaming
and descrying dreams in the eye of his leader.

But Sir Keith, staring round at his leader, somehow
altered and became Adam Smith! And
Smith turned into a stockbroker! 'How – ?'
The broker broke in: 'Of our band…
except those engaged on defence…anyhow
of the rest the centre is me; I stand
for the essence, the mechanical entrails of video-
age Tory. I take it you intend
to ask about Howe. He's in the boot,
where we want some solid weight. Indeed a
colleague on Foreign in this dream's contraband.'
And lambent the beam in the eye of the leader.

He lied for his leader: 'Where misery *is*
it's incurable. There's no cure for our ills
where the land isn't fertile. This
you yourself would say. Your sort tills
poverty's ploughlands. It's paralysis,
dead seed sown into soil that kills
it twice over.' I told him: 'You must miss
on your video half what I *will* say: that spoils
our discussion. Let's not scorn all the skills
of free barter; but chance – that's the breeder
of this mess. This national murrain muzzles
me; and so does the eagle eye of your leader.'

V

In lieu of the leader – who vanished, smiley-eyed –
that essence, the new Adam, that *éminence grise*,
turned icily, like a teacher who's tried
n times to explain the economic freeze.
'Look through the window at the world that has died
under your sentimental socialism. The Tories
have the perfect pearl, our policy.' Beside
me the seat shone, so that the trees
took a gleam from the glowing. I saw poverty's
sad spirits amid the slim trunks.
'Whose ghosts are these?' 'Whose? Oh, aren't those
the idle, the dull, the deprived, the drunks?'

To muddle the dull and the desperate and indigent
argued not that anyone had an arrogant heart
but that gentlemen are gentle and generally so eminent
they propose Sir Pretentious Privilege, Bart –
this stockbroker, ally and co-agent
of the merciless morals of monetary art –
to act as example, an astute accountant,
to a meddled-with nation. 'We must make a start

somewhere,' he said. 'The prosperous have first part
in the likely prosperity. Let the lower ranks
labour for it; and let *them* live apart
from the idle, the dull, the deprived, the drunks.

Liverpool's slums, Lambeth's… the dull haunt
our labour markets; they must live monastic
lives until the industrious, the investors, the brilliant
and expert haul us on stretchy elastic
towards wealth.' We whisked by the scant
foliage; finally the faint tick
of the Bentley puttered through a gap; the pennant
waved in an autoroute's wind; then as quick
as changing channels, we chased in fantastic
acceleration along the high banks
of the motorway, meditating our majestic
escape from the dull, the deprived, the drunks.

'Those who are disloyal, dull or leftist
can't be argued with,' came the down-my-nose-
pours-contempt-for-the-wet-collectivist
tones of the broker. 'Any true Briton knows
the battles of Brixton were a left-wing ameliorist's
feeblest hour: first he allows
free rein to the rabid immigrationist
and, then, terrified at race tension, throws
borrowed money at the fighting that follows.'
'Are you a peggiorist, then?' 'That's the punks
and sick-minded. Only we *cure* the sorrows
of the idle, the dull, the deprived, and the drunks.'

The dull concrete didn't narrow with distance
as parallels ought; with no vibration, the v-8
lightly-stressed engine gave no sign of advance
down the blind, hurtling roadway. At this rate
we travelled on, talking as in a trance,
while false video reception made us late

though on time with each ready response. Then a giant's
soft pantomime hat appeared over the exit
sign to a services station. 'Wait,'
shouted this hirsute hitch-hiker. If my monk's
robe was threadbare, his fustian was fit
for Idle Jack, Dull Dick, and stage drunks.

VI

This was the dull giant, *Want* – Idle Jack
would prove his partner – he was gasping for air
in his ill-kempt heights, coughing with cardiac
troubles from carbohydrates, a ragged tear
in his doublet, bearing a child on his back.
Sir Pretentious huffed as we passed that despair:
'He can't compete: he hasn't the knack
of self-mobility; in our mercy we care
for the weak but wet-nursing by welfare
won't solve his problems: our priority is the average…
to upper-average; and afterwards care
for Giant Number One of those named by Beveridge.'

A 'Diversion' swept us into a giant slum
area where drifts of ancient dirt
stirred in the curbsides and soiled every room.
Beside high-risers, kids called as if hurt
in their gullets; one gaped as aghast as a dumb
man mauled by a lion; a militant squirt
of spit from another in an infant's nihilism.
His mother's broad bottom bustled her skirt,
plumped out on poverty; like an incestuous flirt
she cuddled a skeletal grandmother, savage
in extreme *Squalor*. The Bentley took a spurt
past Giant Number Two of those named by Beveridge.

We drove by a dried-out fountain, its giant
stone basin wreathed in weeds. As our

Bentley stole past the Job Centre's spent
offerings, cat-calls were coming from every colour
of ethnic minority: dusky Moslem, defiant
PNP Blacks, punks with purple hair,
red Irish, brown Indian… in fact, every tint
from China to Cockaigne crowding round to pour
an inner city scorn on me; a spinning flour
bag carried right through our ethereal carriage
walls, while I smiled wonderfully as though saviour
of *Idleness*, Third Giant of those feared by Beveridge.

'Regrettably, a number of giants roam
our land,' groaned the broker. 'All born identical.'
But a baby giant, abandoned by adultdom,
sat by the roadside ahead, a shackle
like a criminal's on his ankle. He was one on whom
innocence and incapability impose an immutable
Buddha face beaming; for Down's Syndrome
which places in eyes such a permanent chuckle,
had kissed him with mercy. My passing, meanwhile,
threw dust on this infant, *Ignorance* – at the edge
of welfare, you may meet the mild eyes of the mongol,
and of Giant Number Four of those named by Beveridge.

We passed into putrid smoke, the pageant
of giant abuses perhaps over; a stupor
engulfed me; I eyed some effulgent
steam leaving my lips like a super-
luminous illness; an inner irritant
penetrated my lungs from the pea-souper.
A hospital porter loomed up: 'No patient,'
read its sign, 'admitted unauthorized. We recoup a
part of our expenses from private groups.' A
nod from the broker: 'It's not just the rich:
better to combine against *Disease*. We have BUPA
to fight Giant Number Five of those named by Beveridge.'

VII

Inside the pollution a police sergeant spotted
us and stopped the blue Bentley, not on Sus
for we were above suspicion. We started
gliding from the slum as he guided us
out on the freeway toward our allotted
destination – Steel City – as detritus
blew free from the bonnet. But the cuffs
of my gown were wet with blood. Worse,
my mind rained into my heart at my callous
and inactive embitterment. Empty pity
made me shrink from the broker or return mute animus
as from Hazard Country we sped to Steel City.

Blotting the blood with some Baldwin-era Hansard
pages that I found in a fresh folder
beside me, I began inspecting the tarred
surface vanishing fast under us; from old
repairs and bumps, the Bentley bit hard
on a shimmering grey straight; it yelled a
gale, tyres roaring, as we raced toward
that shining city on a far hill's shoulder.
Past crumbling factories, or convents far older,
we kept after that upland vision, whose clarity
depends on distance; it grew colder
as from Hazard Country we sped to Steel City.

'To hazard a guess at the thoughts in your head,'
cautioned the broker, 'if we could only create
jobs out of thin air, then we would' – though as he said
this he was speaking out of thin air, that
is, he'd become a mere shadow and ahead
of me seemed out-of-synch in his video state:
fast rewind, flutter, cut dead.
'May I explain for a moment: we get
jobs that when a definite delivery date,

price, and goods we produce fit the
needs of our customers…' I stared at his seat,
as from Hazard Country we sped to Steel City,

for he too had vanished; the old Hansard file
lay open and I almost believed that Baldwin
himself was now speaking wonder woman style:
'I'm not the one who's responsible when
people in jolly good jobs strike…' At this denial
something glinted on the English hide seat between
me and the door: a dull whitish pearl
of the size and opalescence of a spring onion,
newly shaped. The chauffeur shot me a grin.
'It's an old disappearance dot from TV
history. It's our warrant, our will to win,
as from Hazard Country we speed to Steel City.'

On the hilly horizon of Hazard arose
a non-liberal city of stainless steel
tilted towards us, trembling like a spring whose
destruction wrought outwards but whose real
rage was central. Dante's rose
had been superlative, swift and still,
but this was more like the maze of Minos,
chief justice of chaos' capital,
its centre fixed in the fierce free will
of capitalist entrepreneurs, its peripety
a doorless wall against the weak. Yet still
from Hazard Country we sped to Steel City.

VIII

Ascending to the capital of Hazard Country,
I saw cornfields spread out like sandpaper squares
beneath us. A little Britain; its boundary
encompassed by my eye; an island of cares

made solvent by oily seas. Our Bentley
halted by a high city wall that Bill Sirs
would have been proud of: steel, polished to buggery,
a stainless satin finish like 'Where's
the flaw in perfect polish?' There was
a 'magic eye' in the mirroring precipice
of metal, one blind to paupers and borrowers.
My false pearl paid the price

of entry: its falsity educated the 'eye'
whose photons suddenly thought themselves wrong,
misled by the selfishness of mirrors and by the lie
of bad timing beamed at them along
the rays from the wrong pearl, reflected by
the steel. The wall opened; we slid in among
shining shops and de Chirico sky-
scrapers. We could hear the ringing song
of Christians in a metal cathedral, whose long
curve of steps climbed to the iris
in a door like a lens, where loitered a throng
of girls. Their false pearls paid the price

of entry to false fame. They were snapped up by a
huge Canon – the camera, that is, –
formed like St Paul's. Though I seemed a friar
in my gown, I was actually more of an atheist
but was snapped by the iris and came to in the choir.
That lot were journalists and looked even less honest
than me: silk-suited, silk-faced like a Blackfriars
drinking den after deadline, their diarist
eyes on the swivel. I was intoning some eucharist
hymn about salvation without sacrifice
of the class system, hyped by a sensationalist
press whose false pearls paid the price

of entry; and I was now a newsman as false
as any on the Street. Steely light

slanted past slotted columns, for the cathedral's
were like camera spools, splendid in spiritual night.
The congregation in black, except for the girls,
who were lambs round the altar rails and wore white
Princess Di wedding dresses. 'Sundry earls'
heiresses,' I assumed, seduced by the sight
of the sub-Royal served up to write
about in some gossipy piece paying lip service
to Royalty as spectacle, rubbing up the right
way an editor's false pearls, the price

of my entry to by-lined falsity. The Bishop,
from the Diocese of Deference, had been
round with the wafer course already; the cup
approached and although awake in a dream
I closed my eyes and supped a sweet syrup
while conformity cooed overhead and the canteen
passed onward. I sensed that to sup up
such class sentiment was an unclean
act and I was heady from it. I had to lean
on a neighbour for support. Yet I felt nice,
full of hauteur, high on decency – but obscene,
for my false pearl paid the price

IX

of entry. A false sun in the soaring
metal cupola melted the manifold
of my dream-time; the dome, speckling
like some television wipe, spilt gold
coins which cascaded down into crawling
heaps. Those valuable virgins, bold
of this privatization of spiritual striving,
tore off their muslin and – like me, taking hold
of the coins – jammed them just where old
Danae discovered you could day-dream a fuck

from hard money. My self-image swelled
as I left and strode out on the Street of Good Luck.

Ego inflation on that egoists' street
was for wealthy Members only it was only too evident.
Two jobbing brokers blanched at my state.
'I thought we were working on nought per cent,'
spluttered one of those experts, consulting his slate.
On a farther hill the proud 'I' of Parliament
arose by the river and its tower had a great
Wheel of Fortune for Big Ben, as if government
meant ruling the City, the Exchange and the Mint
by the hope that a fall of the hands on the clock
would land on lucky six; a hell-sent
inversion of values on the Street of Good Luck.

Behind me a section of street sank in
as the phony cathedral collapsed, amortized
in its own sinking fund of spiritual in-
solvency. The girls staggered out like squised
cats – Chelsea cats for they'd shed their muslin
and appeared Zandra'd up for supper, apprised
of liberated fashions to feed the famine in
their Tory hearts. Not truly politicized
they scattered, hoping some husband-sized
financier would be waving a wallet so thick
that female and funds would fuse in a high-rise
high-yield stock on that Street of Good Luck.

Stalking the street, erect with that stuff
about royalty and religion and ready
to fornicate with Fortune's feminine staff,
I loped after a likely lady,
friar though I was and wearing such rough
clothing. Her carefully-cut Rasta-thready
blonde hair, her wily nether half
filled me with: sex = self-will = speedy

orgasm = self-aggrandizement = 'Steady
on, I am the dreamer and can dream up suc-
cess that's worth more than a wallet. Already
you've gathered *my* gold on the Street of Good Luck.'

The next bit's a mystery: mistreating a woman
 – not even the abuse of another's soul –
hadn't any tie-up with Tories; but the terrain
of chance, of Steel City, and the whole
theme of false values now ran
through my loins like lust; I stole
up behind the blonde, crowed like a bantam,
didn't go for a posterior goal
but entered her top to toe. A coal-
blackness blotted out her silk back
and I reeled in an utter reversal of role:
all good turned to bad on that Street of Good Luck.

X

On that street sex was one-sided and sterile,
an inversion of self-image on its own image
as Dante was drawn through the dark navel
of Satan. My face froze frig-
idly like a demonic id whose idol
is itself in its stony enjoyment of rage.
My stomach tried to turn over to tell
me it was a happy puppy, but the passage
turned me entirely, eventually to emerge
at the woman's front, facing her, faint
with despair to have done such self-damage.
She said softly, 'Follow your Saint.'

In the following instant I thought that the fortune-
hunter's blonde hair had
become a rich red and that Rosine

herself, whom *I'd* been hunting, now stood
before me, her russet robe a ruin,
her face all frowns, her fair eyes sad
at the vicious violation of virtue in
my pretended acts of love, my perverted
rape of the rosy pearl whose red
was talismanic – a truth without taint.
In this single instant I realized what she'd
suffer if I followed the feet of my Saint.

For my blood flowed upward to beat on the barrier
of the spiritual; and I saw into Rosine's soul –
it screamed like an oyster in hysterics, the inner
sanctum slimy. But a shining idol
lay within the lining, tiny, dreamier
than Buddha; it was the beaming baby mongol,
Ignorance. Immediately, I felt calmer.
The rosy saint of all sexual, all social
polity had appeared in her soul. The pearl
seed of her Socialism was this subnormal infant.
The soul was screaming, suffering my evil
violation, but the voice said, 'Follow your Saint.'

All I saw was her soul and, following that, Rosine
herself couldn't be dreamed of concurrently:
just this jewel, this joyful, serene
jot of the former giant, though ignorantly
deprived, become all I desired, the divine
baby-being in non-being. Fervently,
I sought to stabilize the ignorance, but the scene
was blurring. As it blanked out, the Bentley's
silver-blue sidled up silently.
Inside was the silky-backed blonde, her serpent-
like Rasta-threads wreathed quite reverently
into saintly halos, so that 'Follow your Saint'

meant 'Follow this Medusa'. My mind
was still bathed in babydom, but
the woman awaited me. She was some kind
of secretary now, all pencils, sorting out
parliamentary papers. I was an M.P., my suit lined
with plum-red – the gown had gone – ; no doubt
I was Labour – of the lunched-at-Locketts, dined-
at-Whites variety, never without
this personal assistant, and set up to spout
for party and people, proud that Parliament
had seduced me. I sat down beside her to scout
out a refuge from innocence, from 'Follow your Saint'.

XI

We followed the river to Fortune's Wheel
and its Parliament, then down an underpass
with metal surfaces, spinning like a steel-
coiled worm-hole through time, whereas
we held steady as a spaceship in a special
effects catastrophe. My secretary was
proffering my Order Paper as though political
protocol prevailed in whirlwinds. Pompous
because the Bentley was mine now and because
the main motion before the Parliament
was mine also, I stared in surprise
at the annoying frivolity of an amendment –

'annoying', as I was aiming at a veto
of Margaret's money measures with a motion
of censure: 'That this House has no
confidence…' and so on. The Opposition
leader would come first, but a clever cameo
performance, well-reported, would promise me promotion
chances: just my luck if some shallow
ass threatened our forcing of an election

wording the anonymous, a-logical alteration
that: 'Parliament places no confidence in Parliament'.
As if one could *confidently* call into question
oneself? An annoyingly frivolous amendment.

Lost in the annoyance I was hardly aware
we'd been grounded in a gravy-brown, gothic
décor. From the car door a corridor,
panelled in oak, opened an honorific
progress down a carpet in the Commons. My career
was poised on the pure *realpolitik*
of the day's debate. The doors to the Chamber
were pulled open by the body politic
of the Sergeant at Arms and I saw seraphic
gleams of light. But a grey garment
floated by me and I almost forgot to think
of my motion and its annoying amendment.

Annoyance gone, I saw my grey gown
sported by an old M.P., pass by us
en route for the opposite lobby. My own
feeling was I should follow, that impulse
being stopped by my secretary – she'd shown
me my speech draft. I stuttered, 'This is serious:
who was that man?' 'Well, he's been known
from here to eternity as "Father of the House",'
she sneered. 'But Shinwell, who's a scrupulous
Lord, is no sell-yourself Socialist bent
on crossing the Commons in a confidence crisis,
when we're up against such an annoying amendment,'

I argued, anxious instead of annoyed,
for the 'Father' had resembled my father,
drained and grey, descended to that void
from which he waits for me to remember
him in dreams. Through the doors that candid
light reminded me I was a Member

of the assembly, one unable to avoid
being beckoned by ambition. To enter
the Chamber changed me entirely. A sheer
bombardment of light blazed on the Government
side where *I* was! All was wrong. But whoever
had added the previously annoying amendment,

XII

could annoy me no more. The light
that flooded the Government side of the Floor
shone from a white world opposite
whose crystal cliffs crowded the shore
of a fast-flowing stream. This was the trite
stream of time that I've talked of before,
unusual here in issuing in spate
from sluices set under the Speaker's chair.
The Commons was cut in two: the corps
of M.P.s from all parties packed close
together on the Government benches, and that gladder
kingdom whose cliffs were clear glass.

The glassy surfaces gleamed with fragmentary
mirrorings of all the M.P.s, as we peered
at a cliff-like façade like a stacked factory
for industrial ice whose cubes reared
up winking in sun from an unseen clerestory.
And the sun was Switzerland-warm; it speared
across narrow alleyways, silvery-rosy
as a laser lancing through weird
chunks of Turkish Delight. It cheered
my heart, empty as that heaven was,
for the normal confusion of the Commons had cleared
in that other kingdom whose cliffs were of glass.

Like a Douglas Oliver look-alike
the Speaker dreamily searched our side

and 'recognized' me, which although autoscopic
for both of us, deepened the dark divide
in myself. I stood up to speak,
conscious of the stream swirling through the wide
middle-ground of debate, a dike
between self and supreme. I couldn't decide
what stage we were at in the motion, but I'd
read Aaronovitch on the A.E.S.
so I started magnificently, like a sinner who defied
a heavenly kingdom where the cliffs were of glass.

I glossed over Margaret's giant, *Inflation*:
wages were hiked when unions pushed
hardest; this, helped by a hapless nation
whose purchasing exceeded production, pushed
up prices; then the pound's depreciation
pushed up import prices, and that pushed
up not just prices but the expectation
of price rises to come, which pushed
up purchasing demand – then the wage push would
renew: it was 'who pushed who', if alas
you plumped for the policies the Tories had pushed.
I called this across to that kingdom of glass.

Each glassy fragment flashed a vignette
of some vinegary visage beside me, famous
in Cabinet, Shadow Cabinet, Bennite,
or SDP-Lib circles; so as
I explained the monetary answer, I expected
the common Commons mix of raucous
attack and counter-attack; and yet
reflected in facets of the bevelled surfaces
was a sort of solemn, sourpuss
musing, like orang-utans *en masse*,
except for the pearly premier's face
quizzing me hard from the kingdom of glass.

XIII

I lambasted the class basis of this blatant
war on workers, those job losses which
were a deliberate disciplining, with decadent
fiscal fiddling to facilitate rich
investments abroad and to add to arrant
social disparity at home. 'We must switch
to expansion, power-sharing with the potent
multi-nationals, a new package
of nationalization…' Bennites and Aaronovitch
had proposed planning agreements, provision
for welfare, etc., but I stopped, such
a woman I saw walking in the unworldly kingdom.

The windows of that world shone as they opened
at her passing; her compeers in the sans-pareil
surely hid in the cliffs, their heightened
purity transparent: Rosine's apparel
was royal red, a red brightened
by the crystal country which, like Campari
running through ice, her progress reddened
as she turned and re-entered my reverie.
Like the lost lioness – not the Tory
roary British lion but a better emblem,
a more lithe, love-like beast – she
walked shoreward in that unworldly kingdom

to confront the Commons from the world of clarity.
I recognized Rosine the way you'd recognize
your lover's look in union as a unity
if you won your way inward to where her eyes
have sent contrary signals to the quiddity
of single sight. She doubly symbolized
both lioness and pearl: lioness in agility
pearl in the setting of an immobile paradise
made active by her movements. In medieval guise,

she'd denote Mercy, the divine *donum*;
secularized, she was Socialism, this wise
woman walking in the unworldly kingdom.

She stood by her world's deep shore,
her red raiment baubled with pearls;
others hung in her tawny hair or
braceleted her wrists; a rope of those jewels
gave her gown a girdle, and she wore
sandals as sparkling as a little girl's.
Many wanted to join her, whether
rightist or leftist, but the rapid whorls
of the river ran between us. The curls
of her head were adequate coronal for the Common
People's royalty; yet nothing so regal as
this woman walking in the unworldly kingdom.

Her speaking stole through our world with a spatio-
temporal delay: I definitely heard
her but what I clearly came to know
was the voiceless knowledge of some quick word
that grips my attention as I gradually go
off to sleep – voice and knowing not severed
like the temporal tricks of the Bentley's video
yet knowing a wit-stroke behind the revered
word. And I ached to be whole-hearted
about it and always encountered the phantom
time-lag between the truths uttered
by this Saint walking in the unworldly kingdom

XIV

and my world. 'The unpopulated whiteness
surrounding me,' Rosine reluctantly began,
'casts light from an ideal land – the place
where I'm exiled, since your exiguous island

won't pay the price of the pearl. It's of less
value when removed from the Real, but I can
stay for a few years only in a virtueless
nation, or mated to some magniloquent man
whose ambition rides high on the alternative plan
of the T.U.C. Don't you see
your unfunded promises could prove falser than
the false pearl of the premier's policy

that you've spent so much spite in politically blacking?
Did Labour, with Wilson, show the down-the-line
courage to win on the wage front? Did Jim
Callaghan grapple with a single, genuine
solution to the seventies' gradual slacking
that the radicals didn't reject? To undermine
is *so* bloody radical that it leaves all the rootless attacking
the roots.' 'Order!' roared the Tories. 'Resign!'
roared the radicals. 'This isn't our Rosine,
this isn't Socialism.' 'This isn't even seemly!'
countered the Conservatives. And some: 'It's a sign
that there's more false pearls than the premier's policy!'

'Virtue is vulgar; there's no politic
pretension of phrase in my prescient domain
where the voice of the poor is the voice of the rich
as high in aspiration as the Harrovian,
Oxbridgean, Union Soc., wealth-thick
velvetone of a Commons status-vulgarian,'
retorted Rosine, with uncommon rhetoric.
'Until you can also condemn the also-ran
horse-tail-wagging-the-head, trade-union-
inspired, internecine, leftist sycophancy
in a style fit for it, the state is stuck
with a Tory for pearl and a falseness for policy.

The warm heart, when weak, is politically unsound
and even Conservative Christian courage

like that of your father is sounder. He'd have found
it spineless the way you welcome the wreckage
of monetarism, omitting to mention that, drowned
in liquidity, the whole western world sees that wage-
based, spend-your-way-out platforms are bound
to fail eventually. A fine rage
you pretend at Tory "cuts" when your page
is blotted with careless schoolboy accountancy!
It's the people have paid for your go-brokerage
which has lacked the pearl, some policy

of courage. The policy pushed through by your premier,
though bad, was believed in. Not yours. But
no, you resist these thoughts, thinking them far
too unradical, and you undemocratically undercut
the roots of all politics by packing the Labour
echelons with economic dreamers; and the electorate
is supposed to think wishes are pearls. Where are
those who will learn the lesson? Not
Tory cruelty – fight that – but if a vote
goes monetarist you must work for it, until mercy
mists the eyes and the majority doubt
no longer that the pearl is false. Her policy

XV

then, through the premier's persistence will police
the State back to Socialism, for it's who's who
looking after who's who, what's called "extremist" –
though it lets the poorer half learn what you're up to:
not a gentleman Tory gerrymandering consensus
by wooing the affluent worker to a "something blue"
morganatic marriage, where all marital status
would go to the "wet" Tory spouse.' This view
of Margaret and her monetary ministers was too
benign for my Bennite belligerence. I rose

to interrupt and Rosine withdrew
by walking the shore, her sandals in the shallows.

'Shall we allow this Socialist spirit,'
I asked, 'privileged in her palatial,
ice-cold dawns, to disinherit
her followers in this forum with her unreal
centrism?' (The side of her skirt had a tear; it
was as if my words whipped age on her, a weal
of grey skin was scored where the cloth parted.)
I went on: 'We're worried about real
incomes, real indigence, really unequal
national shares; no soft-nosed
kindness to all comers, no universal – '
She stopped on the shore, her sandals in the shallows.

'The centre's not shallow,' she sighed, 'all you said
lashed at my flesh, made my heart fail
and my spirit grow old; when the Grail has fled
the grey creeps over the realm, yet you rail
against any national unity naked
enough to bear offspring, for you a betrayal
of a Marxist revision that would wed red to red
in a bed become barren. Believe this: the Grail
is a mystery for *me*, a union of male
and female in fruition. Maybe something glows
in a centre of birth, very deep, a changed soul...'
She stayed on the shore, her sandals in the shallows.

Shallow water wet my feet
while the same water wet hers which wore
the wavelets like colourless footwear – fit
galoshes for such sandals. The more
I gazed the quicker time's oar beat
down a river running without a roar.
She let me look at her; the glassy light
that shone across from that crystal shore

cast a greying glamour on to the floor
where the Commoners crowded together, our rows
frozen into silence, our stillness the sculptor,
as she stopped on the shore, her sandals in the shallows.

'These shallows,' she said, 'show us the way
to judge the extreme; it's only one edge
or the other of the fast-flowing play
of the river purling between us in a passage
so swiftly exact that nothing can stay
its course; it careens by the clear verge
of my world like a wasting away
of potential perfection. The ideal cannot purge
your chamber of Thatcherism: no thaumaturge
can cure a thaumaturge. Follow those
who keep to the centre current of courage.'
She spoke sadly, her sandals in the shallows.

XVI

Beyond the shallows the stream's sinews
wrestled beneath black gum:
what was so swift was still, whereas
the depths drove ever onward. Dumb
and motionless, the M.P.s seemed to muse
like beached oarsmen bum by bum
under the balcony beams of a boathouse
 – for the cutting-off of the Commons gave it some
such affinity with the river flow. From
afar, I saw a steely sheen,
a patina on the profile of the TV P.M.,
as the river ran so rapidly between

Rosine and this premier – not iron as the Press
allege but an adman's alloy of steel
and pearl. If a TV's phosphores-

cence fails, satin-finishes steal
into brightness and burnish the bones of a face.
So now a gathering greyness gleamed in the pearl
features of all our faces – yes,
faces of steel. Furthermore, the ideal
heroine was altering, ageing, in my still
enfeebling dream. The facial skin
of Rosine was begrimed with grey in a gradual
decrepitude. The river ran rapidly between

us and, at the age-lines that ran through the ashen
remains of Rosine's once-rosy appearance,
I was horrified; in my hot heart I began
to examine at last that excessive reliance
I'd place in attacking the Tories; and
it came clear I was caught in a frantic trance,
one in whose heartless debates no woman
premier had acted; only the adman's
lying image. I looked askance
at the steely leader and knew what I'd seen
was no Thatcher but one of my own dream's creations.
Then the river ran so rapidly between

Margaret and Rosine that my eye ran with its
depths and returned reluctantly to the red
gown by the shore. But the garment's gussets
were growing grey; the colour had fled
from the skirts, and, scattered in singles and bits
of girdle, the pearls pebbled the bed
of the river. That fair face in fits
of ageing altered before my astonished
gaze. The gestures were jerky in the pallid
robe: the regal form of Rosine
shrank and her straight spine doubled
as the river ran rapidly between

the cracked crone, who ran cackling back
from the shore, and me, her ashamed supporter.
Those crystal cliffs had become grey rock –
the sempiternal as senile. The Thatcher
followers shone brightly as they sat stock
still: heads still steel, their suits a
polished pearly sheen; each back
mirrored the front in a vice-versa
as if *ego et me* might be sister or brother
twins, like meaning *all* you mean
mightily in a worship of will without a
blemish. The river ran rapidly between

XVII

those rivals and the crone, Rosine, who ran,
doubled, into a darkening, door-like cliff;
and it cracked apart and closed again,
its granite surface shook as if with
the honour of receiving her. Once a heaven,
that aged world was no longer worth
a dream; the stream had grown Stygian,
its waters oily. Full of offal, not swift
as before; and the Commons blanked out, because if
the ideal is lost, the real also loses
its iridescence; in the eye itself
a politic blindness, not pearly roses.

In the blind gap between dreaming, my bed
groaned and the grey gown writhed as I tossed
and turned, tormented, since all that I wanted
had waned at the word, 'courage'. I almost
awoke, feeling empty and isolated,
continuing the debate with a departed ghost.
But the dream survives between dreams in the red
furnace within and the black frost

without, this double denizen lost
but refound when the live heart unfreezes
a country's Conservative night at its coldest
and in politic blindness bloom pearly roses.

Blindness of spirit had beggared my vision;
its duration that night I shall never know.
Finally I felt a hand on the crimson
cuff of my gown. I came to, and although
dreaming was blind in the dream. 'Ash on
an old man's sleeve,' someone thought; somehow
the phrase was a parody; for my father's cremation
that I'd attended ages ago
left ashes, not this corpse to clutch at me so
by the gown's red cuff which for me I suppose is
like wearing his heart on my sleeve, as though
in the blindness of ashes could bloom pearly roses.

Yet I seemed like a blind man led by another,
stumbling in sand; and I sensed that the Eliot
thought had been my own thought, for my father
now spoke, in death still a typical Scot:
'Please yourself with all this palaver
about Socialism; the cemetery is certainly not
a Tory stronghold. The truth is, I'd rather
your Socialism shone with your past; you're not shot
of that fatherly honesty, walk humbly but
remember your innocent days; who refuses
his childhood's a booby – and I haven't forgot
your politics, with its blindness and pearly roses.'

The blindness began to clear but I saw
we were stepping through sand flecked with ash
which clung to my feet as we followed the shore-
line of a rapid river. On a rash
impulse, I faced my father before
I was prepared for his pallor and I wish

I had not, for he fainted and fell to the floor.
When I knelt, there was ichor under his eyelash;
he was grey-gowned, red-cuffed, but his sash
was gold. I held him, held him as close as
I could and prayed for his Scottish courage
to place in my blindness a promise of roses.

XVIII

Lightning blinded me; in the thunder I embraced
ash, and would have kissed ash if I could,
for the flesh fell apart into cinders. The past
would not give me kiss for kiss, though the good
in it flurried the ashes into life. Amazed,
for I again wore the gown, I gaped as each cloud
chased after cloud and discharges raced
into the earth where I knelt; I knew that I viewed
swift time from its crystal shore; then I stood,
unharmed, armoured, as it were, in the old
gown but unable to gaze at a new flood
of light from crystalline cliffs flashing gold.

For the littoral was laved with light as a band
of grey-gowned friars gathered by my side
and a company of nuns came along white sand
in processional; I matched them stride for stride
like the past passing, ashen, through the land
of ideals. I faltered, for suddenly I'd
a presentiment that these were post-Falkland-
take-up-the-Task-Force Tories and alongside
Kinnock-clever, clothe-what-you'd-hide-
in-rhetoric Labourites; yet it's lovely to behold
whatever is wise and all were wise-eyed
under light from crystalline cliffs flashing gold.

The women wore veils but once when the light
raked us a face of sisterly reverence

smiled at me. It was my secretary, who in spite
of all that I'd ventured forgave me. Like virgins
entering God's city the nuns crowded tight
together under the glare, grave pilgrims
to a precipice ablaze. Unimaginably bright
a golden axe glanced down from the heavens
and clove the cliffs into two immense
diamantine doors. On that dazzling threshold
played a mongol baby. Its babbling was *Ignorance*
in light from crystalline cliffs flashing gold.

Light went spiralling sideways through solid
clearways of glass as one great door
opened and all walked humbly ahead;
the pearl that provided so signal an honour
was *Ignorance* – and him just an innocent kid!
I took him in my arms with just as much awe
as Rosine had aroused when young and splendid,
and believed I was the baby, he my progenitor.
He chuckled and a cheerfulness I had never before
experienced now entered my heart as his bold
eyes, so sunny, surprised my deep store
of light. The crystalline cliffs flashed with gold.

In an interval of fulgurous light, in an
instant when the baby gurgled, all the glass
scythed sideways. I had glimpses of spun
barley-sugar passages studded with sapphires,
fit pathways for the now-modest procession
of silent M.P.s; but my own progress was
an arc across the immediate, as again
in an instant I was inside the cliff. And found darkness.
However, a window glowed weakly, about as
scintillating as a cigarette lighter when some old
codger won't get its refill of gas.
The light so much less than those cliffs flashing gold.

XIX

Behind me the background was probably lit
by the passageway; I sensed that the M.P.s
came to surround me. Certainly it
was no time to turn round, for a touch on my sleeve
told me my father'd returned: I would forfeit
his guidance if I glanced at him. Giving me his
arm in a kindly way he confided:
'No, you're not to know: she's
not how you remember her. Eh? Rosine's
the person I mean.' He began to mutter:
'A nation must know its own ignorance. Now gaze
where that window glows beyond a gutter.'

In the empty window appeared an elderly
woman whose shoulders were wrapped in a shawl;
her framed face, lit faintly, looked fairly
stupid, her surroundings – a funereal
terrace – were like what you normally
discover old dears in, in all
inner city slums. She hardly
bothered to raise her eyes. Her real
disease dwelt in the centre of the ideal
realm. She was Rosine in Rags, in utter
poverty; in her cupped palms was the pearl.
Her window gave on to a grimy gutter.

Through the window she was as pale as a water-
mark as I made an attempt to cry out.
No voice came. I felt a
constraint round my neck and knew I had not
forgot *Ignorance*. This infant taught a
great truth to me: he kept tossing about
in my arms in anguish as if he thought *her*
his mother. My father confirmed it: 'The proud
and the politic pretend to have policies without

this blessed baby. You'd think such butter
would melt in their mouths. Hold out that wee tot
to the window giving on to that grimy gutter.'

Our grey wall of gowns confronted the window.
I gave up *Ignorance* who without breaking glass
entered the frame and flew to the elbow
crook of the crone, like a handicapped Jesus
cradled by a careworn Madonna. Although
the pearl appeared in his hand, in a pious
iconography of orbs, the whole hollow
conformity of creeds seemed but a callous
response to his slant-eyed saintdom. None of us
dared speak, for the scene was changing: wasn't that our
own ignorance now part of the indigent terrace,
whose windows gave on to the grimy gutter?

The window went cloudy, but then its weak light
reddened like a TV returning to colour,
and Rosine snapped on to its screen with a slight
wobble. She was weeping but young once more,
pearl girdled, gowned in rose-white,
and clutching the baby to her breast. 'Your
sentiment's so easy,' said her voice. 'Right
in the ideal's inner sanctum you prefer
a sort of commercial for Christ or for
the politics of set-apart poverty. This is but a
child, of an uncared-for category; you ignore
that this window gives on to your own grimy gutter.

XX

Now watch the window.' Within my ignorance
just one, unoriginal, ordinary thought
became so obvious it couldn't be nonsense;
the Second World War for a moment had taught

my nation to know that Conservative negligence
of poverty weakened the purpose fought
for. The strike-bound seventies, strengthening the difference
in working class hierarchies, caused chaos which brought
half a nation to claim that their own cosy comfort
was the aim of their living at all. The way down
was leftist but nasty: do nothing get nought.
(I groaned, lying down in my grey dressing gown.)

'Does the dream come to this?' A debased King Lear
with a sip of the SDP?' In my anguish
I called this across to the screen. The clear
voice answered me: 'First acknowledge
that the highest human intelligence is a near
relation of ignorance; let language
untwist on your tongues. There's no true idea
of political system; so say so; don't languish
in rent-a-Marx/Margaret rhetoric or relinquish
the winning of wealth to the selfish. Anyone
who works for the poor is the pawn of the rich.
But don't – lying down in your old dressing gown –

lie about serving *this*.' I still stood
in the dream by the gutter among all the grey
gowns as she showed us the child: food
crudded its cheeks; each candid eye
was half closed by the lid giving it a lewd
ogle; the mouth lay wide open with its oyster
slime, a birth-place, both oyster and blood.
The ghost of my father all at once went away
to an immense distance. An intense ray
of midnight from the eyes' centres entered my own
eyes in a black instant of immediacy.
(I gasped as I lay in my grey dressing gown.)

A memory sea that had lain at low tide
in my mind slowly mounted making green

my dense darkness, radiant liquid
filled my vision; somewhere, half-seen
a precious pearl was shining in me; a pellucid
awareness of all that had passed – all that had been
born in me one morning when the mongoloid
eyes of my son stared at me, smiling, serene
in their way – was eerily glowing again, what I mean
by Socialism, that our soul and our selves are unknown
yet unconsciously known in the union between
people. (I lay in my grey dressing gown.)

She said: 'The pearl is ourself in which lies
a rosy reflection of all whom we care for
enough, the Other rendered perfect in a paradise
of our self-love. Unthinkable therefore
to pretend that the poor will profit from policies
whose mercy has greyed in the pearly mirror
of the nation's identity. We should idolize
the giants of Beveridge, make a Britain to cheer for,
a workforce that works for all we are here for
on earth: the self and its soul whether known
in the one or the many.' (My mind full of fear for
that pearl turning grey, I lay in my gown.)

The pearl that lay in the baby's palm
centred all thought and in it my face
enlarged, smiling; I saw the smooth arm
of Rosine round my neck. Then rays
of heartening light, rays of no-harm
shot from my eyes to my eyes. But the space
between us was widening; in alarm
I began crossing the gutter that only grace
can cross. I caught a mere trace
of grey from the gowns, her grave frown,
and awoke in a dawn of our daily disgrace,
lying down in my father's grey dressing gown.

An Island That Is All The World

In honour of Mona
and those closest to me
whose pasts were involved
with these presents

I have to write some autobiographical things; talk about deaths of four relatives; let myself be sent back by deaths to childhood; then return to a middle age of restless moves between England, Paris and New York, never losing the obsessions which began in childhood. But I hope a much wider question will steal into this: what does it mean to talk of spirituality in poetry when no religious belief lies behind the enquiry? An unfashionable question. Avoiding intellectual sophistication, I shall look at the actual occasions of poems to find, not ways of explaining them, but spiritual sources in childish or adult sides of personality. Literary philosophy cannot escape scepticism or programmatic ambiguity about spiritual issues because we are trapped in the web of language, doomed, it seems, to disbelieve in the unity of self and of artistic forms: along with that, goes a loss of spirit. Such theorists are dangerous guides to areas where the poem, on the other hand, can make evident to the simple-hearted: 'This happened – spirit entered language and simultaneously I perceived such and such sights, spoke such and such words.'

> Can't see diesel fumes faze
> from tunnels when the night train's
> ricketing down, carriage fighting carriage,
> on a journey to the past: time in reverse
> leaves no smoke trail behind,
> memory hurries to the birth of kind.
>
> The train shakes badly near home station
> as gales increase, before violent rest
> of very beginning, a destination
> centred in your life again and again,
> perhaps a mother waiting, perhaps a mother dead.
> Once there, a white cloth effaces all ahead.

In middle age, before I left England for Paris, I took the late train from London Waterloo to my mother's bungalow in Bournemouth on the south coast. I think of that night's fierce blizzard as shaking the train's silver harmonica: light in its upper holes, a reverberant buzz. My open carriage was deserted, freezing, and smelt of sour saloons and elderly dust. I sank into correcting a manuscript as we pulled out of London and jolted over the wide crossings. An hour or so later we'd picked up to 100 miles an hour. Then a loud bang, almost thwang, snapped a huge spring and we sickeningly slowed; the lights rapidly dimmed and went out. The windows darted with red sparks flying backwards; whiffs of burning wood penetrated the carriage as we went into a queasy four-mile skid. My mind divided between the calmly pragmatic and the curious. Pragmatic: if we hit a train the bench seats might crush me; so I slid to my knees in the aisle as if praying, but not. My calmness seemed premonitory that I was not about to die. Curious: as the skid continued, I compared the experience to a description of a derailment I'd once written. The whole front of the train heaved and bumped about, an angry Leviathan, shifted to the left, lurched downwards with more thumps, and fell into hissing stillness.

With another passenger I headed for the cab; but the driver, holding his head, was already making his way towards us. He has coped well with the tree that had blown in his path and no-one was hurt. Farce took over. After three-quarters of an hour rescue arrived – far too much of it, multitudes of ambulances, police and fire services. As we negotiated the tall carriage steo down to the track, a public relations man in business suit stood up on the snowy embankment, his voice fading behind us as we trudged in darkness towards ladders on the slope by the bridge. 'British Rail regrets the inconvenience…'. Up top, fleets of ambulances carted us off like invalids to a British Legion hall for tea and biscuits served by volunteers at 2 A.M.

In fiction and dreams I have imagined a train or bus racing through the night; a face appears outside its windows or a rich, calm voice is heard from outside. In this derailment, the fantasy came very near me, a voice born not exactly in the speeding Hampshire countryside but *implied* by my whole life conceived in its unity, yet a voice general enough to be relevant to everyone on the train even if it calmed only me, kneeling there, and almost spoke, comforting me.

When I got home my mother, then aged about 77, told me of the first time my 80-year-old father collapsed playing a round of golf (the second time, he died). She'd been in the garden and at the precise moment heard her name called, gravely and calmly, from the kitchen, 'Marjorie'. So that time such a voice spoke.

The innermost voyager

Jetliners climb above the middle air
of spiritual journeys: flying in dreams
is usually humanized and takes the shaman route
of older beliefs. Once, in a train derailment,
I bore my sense of self so lightly it yearned
for those middle heights. Probably, when dying,
we rise above and see nurses acting in perfect democracy.

We'll not romanticize shamans; but whatever
our job or class there can always be some dream train
where we're squashed in by fuzzy-featured companions;
and one is this other kind, a spirit voyager:
think of a tree bole robed in furs, a wooden bear mask
that nearly speaks. For me, it'd be poets travelling
to a festival, a voice more ancient than ours among us.

We're off to perform our poetry in a noble library,
lodging together, squabbling for bedrooms.
This one in the carriage really troubles us;
he's this great trouble for cleverness,
one who looks as a bear might look if it were a god,
mouth as amused muzzle, head far too large,
blind eyes, great simpleton ears, his suit shaggy.

The carriage wobbles on its bogeys; we spit clever gossip,
exhibit taciturn domination, leftist talk of Gödel's
theorem applied to politics: Fanon's wretched
of the earth will be just that enigma resolved
in the higher social order to come: the talk
soars over famines and floods – hubris like a swank plane
gleaming in the clouds above human geographies.

We're humped about by each other's ambitions.
Frozen Hampshire fields pass by train windows;

there are multitudes of the impoverished
squatting like fir saplings on crusted snowfields,
yellowing sunset as in romance, the figures unmoving.
It's supposed witty to say, 'That view can be resolved
by reference to wider fields of snow, greater poverties.'

Blue-grey shadows mottle this covered heathland
as if a bear's spoor led to whitened hill crests.
The snow's both animal-warm and absolute-zero.
A voice from outside the field of vision, whether
beside us in the carriage or out there in the gliding,
has a warm Hampshire burr, for you perhaps it's female,
for me, the uttermost countryman of my innermost country.

The voice tells how one evening no-one will be safe from cold.
A tree on the line, a loud bang up front, carriage lights dim,
a slowing, windows freckle with sparks, a smell of burnt wood,
and the wrecked express skids four miles with charcoal in its paws.
Then train walls burr terribly but death would arrive
with slow riding and displacement of fear.
Poets would wish their voice warm and fit for such riding.

My middle age seemed new still as a job opportunity opened up in Paris, where, now a teacher, I'd formerly been a journalist. I lived alone in a Paris studio above the hot, roaring Avenue de Clichy. My mother died and then my sister. A time of sea-change after years of stability. Daytime, I taught literature; nighttime, I roamed out with journalists, enjoying the free relationship between men and women temporarily established in restaurants and bars. Later I would smoke a cigar in bed, be warmly drunk, and listen to the tric-trac players crowding round cardboard tables in the street; they fought or shouted protest as a pail of water showered down golden in lamplight from flats above; prostitutes conducted their ballet on the pavement; Brazilian transvestites crowded the cafes; then constant traffic accidents, with police, fire and ambulances screaming off to northern limbs of the city. It was a pleasurable time of self-corruption, and I worried about that before going off to sleep with layers of cigar smoke drifting above my old Apple computer.

A friend drove me out for a swim in a disused gravel pit on the Parisian outskirts. From down in the pit's wide hollow, sand sloped up to hairy green crests, the sky so blue it almost came over the hilltop. Inshore, the lake was stained oak colour but out in the centre, wherever sun geometry didn't brighten the surface, the dark colour of a 17th century chest. My companion set off with a strong sidestroke and I liked watching her progress before plunging in and striking up a crawl designed to catch her up. But she was 12 years younger and the cigars had affected my blood. In the lake's centre, I watched her climbing out on the far side; and discovered I was completely out of stamina. For 20 seconds I flailed about wildly or tried to float, which only made me lose precious breath, and I thought myself sure to drown. She was too far away to help. (We found police notices afterwards warning against swimming there.)

It came to me that the mind must have some hidden rescue of its own. There stabilized within me a steady, confident self, which I imagine to be the self I had often speculated about, the unconscious unity of everything we have experienced and incorporated throughout our length of days, an entity that persists, minutely changing, very minutely, as our conscious self goes through its wilder swings of mood. Much modern linguistic philosophy argues this large entity out of all real existence, but I simply don't believe it. A larger self instructed me to let my limbs do the work while *it* lay back, almost entirely uninvolved. After a great calm – the panic holding off on the periphery – I realized I had ground under my feet, staggered up the shore, and collapsed, as everyday conscious awareness flooded back.

Sometimes I return to the sea scenes of childhood to seek the origins of whatever stabilizes myself in space and time.

The Oracle of the Drowned

Memory in sea-green with sea-weed grain
of glass as the rearing wave rains briefly
before a lot of bother
on the beach of childhood
and men with a burden file across sand.
Those far-out surfaces are lipped
with transparent phrases coming to mind:

that the real dying happened in middle heights
between the lips and the sea floor.
Remember the swim trunks lost in waters
and the first man in our lives who drowned,
this, now, his cortege from the tide-edge,
the scared hanging-down of head and arms
seeing that person's white groin
cooked chicken bared near the hook of the ribs
and a shore-line of horrified children
arrested in their digging to gaze
at seas of such corruption as to change him.
His shirt left behind too long on the promenade rail,
always there in our lives, its caked cotton
fluffy-white in its inner wrappings.
The cloth wandered open at nights as we wondered
what a drowning body could say
when its chest became translucent green,
we courted in our minds such corrupt purity,
never escaping but sinking into not
the unthinkable gift of the self to death,
not the sea flash flood in the throat,
but into the oracle of the drowned;
because the oracle of the dying comes to a halt
but the oracle of the dead continues and has humour in it.
We ask the dying, 'How do you go about drowning?'
and the answer comes first 'I cannot – '
then swims in ambivalent vowels
and voiceless consonants I the washing tide
voiced consonants in the last buzz of the eardrum:
'Aah, I am funtoosh, zooid, walway,
wallowing, rows and rows of waves,
a gooooood on, my sooooul a sea-mew' –
and we learn nothing but the knowledge of pain,
and the hope of a future from it.
But the gone-dead are beamish and talk to us
from out of memory's hollows and gulphs:
'You, boy, in your Bournemouth bed, be with me now

and I will come to you many years later
still drowned in a medium of green liquid
the water whispering through its lips
as the dark whispers to you in caves or before sleep.
And I was a man and had babies
as you, a baby, will have a man and call him "Father"
and as the drowned will have the drowned.'

After my sister died in her mid-50s from liver cancer I flew back to England and helped sort through her belongings, keeping for myself only one early painting and her art college sketchbook. The colour schemes of her oil paintings had changed from the muted greyish-browns of her student work to wilful yellows, mustards, over-cheerful blues and too-sappy greens, with just a grey wispiness reminding you of her earlier days. I associated this over-cheerfulness with a strain in her Christianity which once, for a shaky month, had become messianic.

Her smile constantly expressed goodness and despite spasmodically-ascetic dieting she got fat. She sought out the elderly, infirm and handicapped to help them. At her request during her psychosis I accompanied her to my local church; she made a point of surrounding an extremely-able wheelchair patient with her care. The sermon dealt with St Paul on the Damascus road, but probably only Mona of the whole congregation fully believed in the story, because she was having visions herself. By being a careful confidant and by discussing the relationship between emotion and vision, I was of some help and, with drugs, she recovered. Years afterwards, she asked me if I'd kept in touch with the wheelchair patient and I snapped that I hadn't.

When she got better, her endless hospital visiting, painting of church posters, and attendance at fetes, her simmering passion for the whole clap-trap of social Christianity, still had slight traces of the month of vision.

The time of her dying lay within her power to orchestrate; she'd been a good amateur actress, a genuinely useful skill at such times. She gathered everyone round her at Christmas in my brother's home south of London. On the Sunday of my arrival from Paris, she and I were still planning a trip to Florence, her first, in the New Year. By Wednesday, she was drifting, I thought with the morphine, and we found a wheelchair light enough for me to wheel her round Florence. By Friday, the whole trip had become out of the question.

At communion, on Christmas morning, her last church service, the morphine had left her mouth dry before the hymn. 'God sent me saliva in my mouth so that I could sing,' she said afterwards. She slid towards unconsciousness because of the poisons in her. I took leave, promising to return on the first flight – I thought she had a few weeks to go and was proved wrong. All she wanted to do was make peace with God: 'You can't help me this time.' Not being Christian, I agreed. She tried to thank me and, as I adopted a jokey expression intended to assert my belief in her energies, added, 'You must let me thank you.'

I never quite understood Mona until a memorial service for her. I can't speak for the 600 other people there, but some psychic gate burst open and we were surrounding her. She had felt at risk of divine condemnation and had found her form of salvation: the path had led through slight mania; but it led, let's say, to heaven, or to a greater deserving of such a place than I shall ever achieve.

These words of the quite awful and sometimes wonderful Ramon Lull hold a clue for me:

> Blaquerna enquired of the Truth of his Beloved: 'If in Thee glory and perfection were not that which thou art, what then wouldst Thou be?' And Understanding answered Blaquerna: 'What but falsehood, or a truth like to that of thine, or naught at all, or that in which there would be affliction everlasting?' And Blaquerna said: 'And if truth were not, what then would glory be?' And Memory answered: 'It would be naught.' 'And if perfection were not, what would glory be?' 'It would be that which is naught, or nothingness.'

How does this apply to Mona? Suppose she was driven far into herself by loneliness – having that fatal combination of immense energy, creativity, meticulous memory, emotional inhibition, and occasional long-windedness (a product of the sheer detail of her memory); and suppose this same combination to have been fed by the loneliness. But then, in her isolation fearing divine condemnation, she poured all her denied love into her salvation with such energy that she wrought a highly-coloured goodness, winsome-sweet, religious and eccentric. Well, glory is a necessary part of that, for she aimed so fervently at the Truth in her own vision of it. Though I'm talking to you, Alice, what I'm writing is also set down because of Mona.

Beyond active and passive

'Oh, you are born already!' cries the English mother
in pained surprise to her hanging baby,
as though the finished phrase
had slipped, unfinished, out of an anguish
still continuing, into its adventures.
From before the time when birth was given
babies enter a world of harm.

How suitable for Jains of ancient Bihar
was that Sanskrit middle form,
'I die
unto myself,'
since theirs is a faith of shedding harm
from the solipsism of the journeying soul.

An art teacher, dreamy on morphine, said,
'You can't help me this time,'
as her few relatives
watched her clothe herself for God;
she acted out her death at Christmas
in her Christian counterpart to birth.
Formerly, having no babies, she became
a little religiously dotty, I'd say,
and cared for the elderly
(who crowded her funeral).
Once, when car licence plates coded divine messages
and every lame man was a messianic sign,
on those Damascus roads she called for help
and, needing little, got it.
Sane again, she refound loneliness and service,
living on diets, calorie balances on the dinner table;
her paintings changed from green-browns of college days
to orange-blues of willed bliss;
she talked minutely of those I never knew,
acted the spirit in *Blithe Spirit*,

and died in her Christian language,
'unto Heaven and unto others':
it was the most normal possible thing to do
in the courage of this isolated heart.
Though you cannot do birth for others
but only give it, she gave death to others
by shedding of its harm;
and I think she wasn't born again but born already.

The goldpoint of my whole life is the sketchbook drawing where the boy, reading, looks beautiful in the promise of that luminescent moment. Then I know, too, the boy was beginning the stormy adolescence usual in the 1950s. Not realizing his happiness, he would rage out of his house to go and watch birds on the marshes in Christchurch harbour; in the flight of geese, gulls, herons and smaller wading birds he found the freedom and rhythmic grace that soon were to lead him to poetry and to the mysteries of its stress.

In a poem, each stress is held in memory and perceived as a unity of sound, meaning and special poetic emotion. All durational things on either side of the stroke (the wing-beat) of stress – the length of its syllable, all its sound qualities, what words come immediately before and after it in the poetic line, the whole movement of the line – make us think how weighty or light the individual stress is. The stress centres a tiny island in memory. The centre of the island is occluded; it is the moment when we believe the stress actually happened. We can even strike its instant, a little late, by tapping a finger. If we could bring all those instants fully into consciousness, the poem would become vivid.

We are faced with the ancient question about time: how could we consciously experience an instant of time, when we always conceive instants too late and when an instant can't contain anything at all? Time, self… very small moments of self-experience as portrayed in a sketch… poetic stress: how can we fill this stroke of time which has no duration with meanings and emotions that have? How can an instant and duration be imagined as simultaneous? It's what Christians suppose to happen in the mind of God.

When we try to bring an isolated instant into consciousness, this mystical possibility doesn't occur, because of the tardiness of our minds. We say: the clock has just ticked, I was this kind of self just now or just then, that stress was weak or heavy by an exact weighting. We make in memory a little working model containing the past and future of the moment and, by mental trick, convince ourselves that we experience that model as a present moment. The models are these mental islands of time; and poetic stresses are the smallest clear and complex examples of them I know.

The Heron

I talk only of voices either real or virtual in my ear;
of shadows, only those that pass over islands' sunny turf
vivid to my eye. But when I come to all my birds,
all I've ever seen, they are too many. I talk of things unseen.

Together, they would pack the sky like moving embroidery
in the white silks, browns and blacks of their great tribe,
endless litters of puppies writhing,
a heavenly roof alive but no progress of flight in it.

Every memory adds to this intricate plot;
starting up redshanks first, and they bank, flashing white,
across a sepia estuary where I felt freedom
in watching their undulating patterns on the air.

They flight down but hold at mid-height: horizontal
stick puppets of the Styx. The black light whitens
with the harmonious wings of swan formations,
the day cast over with their bright feathering.

Behind the swans the sky absolutely fills with starlings
homing to roost as once I saw them over Stonehenge;
gulls flock up and hold there, and brown passeriformes
spring between airspaces and stop on invisible branches.

Millions of birds, crows and daws, teal,
quicker wing-beated than wigeon, among mallard hordes;
swifts print arrows on the pulsating featheriness;
the sky is covered over with the puppy litters.

I can't tell you all the names; I'm worried
about the birds rabbling the sky. D'you suppose
I can avoid even the dusty body of every sparrow,
of every sparrow hawk flipping over a thicket?

Unseen , this nature crowds my mind. If there's pulsation,
it's disturbing; if stasis it's a painting
and all the life goes out; but any sudden switch
between pulse and the static is schizophrenic.

In the foreground of the multifarious flights
one talismanic bird, a heron, lifts to the top
of its single leg and takes off like an umbrella.
Fluff in a corner of the past becomes grey flame.

Its shoulders unshackle and heave, legs become the addendum,
the beak stabs out purposefully from the sunken neck.
It sails. In this flight's brevity,
I find what lives for me among all the dead songs.

We never wholly lose our childhood 'immediacy' because immediacy is the beginning of all consciousness. Politicians, boxers, priests and witches know this; they try to gain power over this origin of our identity in their various ways; it's in immediacy and the self-image we glimpse that our sense of our status and moral worth begin, and the politician's 'freedom' is not the freedom we find there.

Michelet's *Satanism and Witchcraft*, bought from an arcade bookstall when I was 14 or so, describes a village girl fleeing the *droit de seigneur*, who couple with Satan in a wood and swells with devilish vapour; she has a brief reign as glittering quean before torture and ignominy. In Michelet's source, Sprenger and Kramer's 15th century Inquisition manual *Malleus Maleficarum*, a witch is seen in a wood with greenish smoke rising from her thighs. I would think up jokes about the chapter headings: 'On the manner in which a sorceress can transport penises through the air in a matchbox'. Once I wondered if a whispered 'yes' was enough to sell yourself to the devil, and whispered it, and had an immediate stab of fear. Such childishness.

Then it's as if one night in Bournemouth Jazz Club a crowd of beautiful blonde girls came down the steps: post-war austerity ended, Scandinavian language students flooded into the town, Espresso coffee arrived, and the generation gap widened. Adolescent sado-masochism, disguised as an interest in the history of witchcraft, matured into more generous understanding of relationships. A 16-year-old insurance clerk, I was waiting in El Cabal for a Swedish girl. For a second I glimpsed something about poetry which seemed profoundly important; then the 'thing' had gone; it's stayed in front of my nose ever since, unattainable like a point in time, the gleam I follow. I saw poetry clear in its act of uniting thought and feeling in immediacy. The stress is the smallest unit in this artistic formation. I believe poetry allows me to glimpse a pre-linguistic mind-state. Philosophy can't trap that belief without deconstructing it; that's why I speak simply about childhood feelings and avoid the language of literary theory. Art gives us confidence that poetic melody shapes emotions and thinking into the one rhythm, a repeatable vivid present; and it feels as if in that alone lie true knowing, true freedom, and true beginning of memory. Imagined poet and imagined reader meet there, in the poem, without the witchcraft of domination.

Witchcraft and torture attack the victim between minute moments of self-consciousness, between the tiny islands; they get through into unprotected immediacy where mind is constantly reborn and they taint its continuity. This can occur with a stab of fear or gradually, as in witchcraft murder: while memories form there is always unconscious immediacy between them, and another immediacy in which they are present, as memories, to the mind. Stevenson has a South Sea story, 'The Isle of Voices', about a warlock who transports himself and his son-in-law by magic mat from Molokai to the beach of a far-off island. There the two of them are, for the inhabitants, just disembodied voices (though it turns out that the spurts' of the wizards' magic fires can be seen by the natives). The shells they pick up become, once home again, silver dollars.

As I pass in a wink from one vivid memory to another I enter newly autonomous unities in mind. Husserl says memory has a closed nature based on the unity of the temporal duration of the original impression which founds the memory. In my own picturing, memory is a temporal island whose centre pulsates with origination and whose boundaries seem secure just until we explore them. What are shells within one island become silver dollars in another; and in the unconscious treasure island of our whole self they become gold doubloons.

These passages divide between childhood and 30 years later. To summarize intervening years: offices, hotels, National Service, journalism including two years in Paris for AFP, mature student in England, lecturer. Family warmths, family deaths. Always poetry. A common sort of life so far. But, during my second time in Paris, separated from all I valued, I lost much sense of the deeper self, which speaks my voice of conscience. Rich harbours of memory became blocked off too and I had to rediscover access to them.

Leaving home island

You don't step out of union but leave home land,
a car door snaps shut at the ferry port;
and it's easy to cross-Channel if gunfire is withheld;
for then the shop runs every night and ceaselessly'
its iron sides heave overhead
knapsacks of students jostle together on docksides
and Port Authority lights illumine girls
you will look at in the saloon, later.
Some word half in sound or memory: the sea could author it,
tongues' yellow slick on harbour mouth waves.

There, in the past, boulders struck dully by a Scottish loch
here, the ferry hull knocking, a bell buoy idling;
there, a dinghy's tarpaulin hauled over a driveway
here, tide across in the bay scrapes down sand;
there, a hissing tap in an echoing kitchen
here, the sea sucking its teeth;
much dear detail you regret having dragged along like chains;
here, the tide pulls stones along metal flanges of the dock;
there, chairs budged on wooden floors downstairs
or workmen dumped a plank into garage foundations
here, cleaners hump about within the lit ferry,
at the gangway's high summit a doorway opens on that light.

You wish to believe a word in your throat;
a word which yields and doesn't break

would moor the present to the past;
yet you must slip away to sea again
like the old-fashioned scoundrel, a pirate,
be a slip hand at escaping by sea swell
on a journey you morally permit yourself
since the fastening, yielding word
can't be spoken. The many sounds
of the populous sea arrive
from an island where voices continue to be.

Under moral tensions in Paris, my psoriasis, which mildly attacks my face and chest, became a little worse. When I called the sketch that of a 'beautiful boy' it's partly the boy's fresh, clear face I thought of. More recently, I read in the New York Times that, when people with multiple personality disorder switch from one personality to another, rashes, welts, and scars may disappear: handwriting, handedness, epilepsy, allergies, and colour blindness may appear or disappear or change. For doctors, it's the power of the mind over the body. In my own poetics, it hints at something else too. I have read something of the modern philosophy of space-time and of deconstructionist literary theory; but I tentatively believe that a pre-linguistic, unconscious 'self', a real creation in space and time, survives the conscious self's dissolution into ever new stages of itself.

The temporal home of this entity is immediacy. Much human behaviour, especially our profoundest moral sense – the simple wish to be 'good' in an undefined way – implies that, unreflectively, people do have this belief. I have no religion at all; I have only tentative belief that the good persists in time.

Multiple personality's strange features seem some evidence of this: there may be an almost autonomous space-time creation of a second or third personality and of a bodily state that accompanies each of them. Something that persists in time but, because of disorder, is imperfectly built into the form of the whole unconscious self like an inappropriate stanza in a poem. In psychosis, this particular area is held in unconscious immediacy until we switch into it. This is why switching is so swift. The, perhaps, our body recognizes that another spatio-tempo region has been entered, and the skin responds to the recognition.

Immediacy is hidden from us by finite mind. The body, its visual perception, and the electro-chemistry of its brain are comparatively crude instruments. If a compass could think, would it believe in the perfect circle? With the two clumsy legs of its argumentative apparatus it would be at a loss to justify its belief except by drawing one as best it could.

The islands of voices

On Saturday, I told myself of the islands of voices.
By today, Sunday, I had lost access.

What happens on the islands?
There are invisibles and the great one
yesterday was my own spirit, revisiting,
betraying my presence by fires that I lit;
they sprang up and died down on the beaches
like dust devils, beside my heel print
which filled with khaki liquid.

Without meaning to,
I've brought many islands to life
and left them there in the sunshine of my dead days.
Hotels, a tall white city in the bay,
or I'm back in Poole, sailing by
a mansion castellated from toilet rolls
guarding Brownsea's neat harbour.
Others are the islands in a child's minute attention,
Idealized, tropical, forested,
Ringed with sand, fringed with white, usual steel-blue.

Revisiting, I saw human forms slipping behind trees;
they could as well have been Pacific figures
on Stevenson's Isle of Voices,
I couldn't hear
if they were ever my companions.
Had I spoken they'd have listened, startled,
receiving the voice like a ball returned
round the corner, to children, by unseen hand.

These are my pasts, these islands
and I'm barred from them by mere turns of mood,
day to day. My own childhoods at play
in their forests, suddenly appeared to me, yesterday;
but shadows dappled the shorelines,
among the birches and elders;
it's hard to match transient feelings
with that precise shadow patterning,
my presence fizzing, flaring up on the beaches.

And today, Sunday, I have lost access.

Separating from England almost cleaved my unconscious identity in half, an irreparable harm I'd done. You wrote to me, Alice, when you were about to fly to Luxembourg where we were both to read at a poetry festival; and we planned for you to stay in Paris with me afterwards. Not the repair but the reconsolidation of my unconscious began then, followed by my present move to New York to be with you.

At rehearsals in the plush little Luxembourg theatre, I had a spot trained on an easel bearing some diagram-cartoons which I show as I read a sequence. The sequence starts in apparent humour but themes of death and politics gradually enter; there's a similar progression in the diagrams. For two days, Italian, French, Belgian, Luxembourgish, English and American poets had performed in a great variety of styles from hilarious music-zen to the chair-up-to-table serious. I knew that our French friend, Jacques, was about to read a sequence concerning the death of his wife and you one about the death of Ted; so I intended to emphasize the humorous side of my diagram-poems – I can read them in many ways. But the theatre's hand-held mikes faded immediately out of mouth-range and the stand-up model I chose rooted me to one place. Also, once onstage I found the diagrams unexpectedly out of reach under their separate spot; and the humorous performance depends upon moving about, pointing out their details. Instinctively, I put my lips near the mike and let my voice softly play with prosody – a purely technical question of stretching out syllables, minutely delaying consonants, altering pitch, timbre, vowel quality, and loudness; I felt nothing, being quite distracted by changing my plans. About halfway through, I noticed my unusual tension, and the audience-darkness was quite still. When I came into the foyer I was shaking, our friend Wendy had tears in her eyes and said, 'How do you manage to go so near that edge?' I wasn't consciously aware I had done so.

The gravity of a poem lies in its whole form, and the prosody alone, being part of that unity, is sufficient access to it without the performer having to feel anything. The whole form lies in the 'unconscious' of the poem; it is its ineffable nature, just as I have a nature developed in me by birth and upbringing. Even if, as I was, we're brought up in some middle-class, snobbish, racist suburb, once we touch more profoundly natural unconscious sides of ourselves all the cultural rubbish falls away and we recognize a deep kinship, an international kinship. We felt such a kinship that evening after you and Jacques had read. As Jacques said, 'It was verray intense.'

For Kind

Kindness acts idly or unnaturally,
leads you into fear. Act in kind.
Kindness makes you idle, worse, unnatural.
Don't be afraid of the darkness of kind;
for it's the birth darkness, vertical twist
of opening lips in the night: life that follows
belongs to you in kind. Don't be frightened
of darkness of origin: it is this darkness,
similar tints of our flesh in the night
of kind. The kind you are, with slim
mammalian chest and, walking to the bathroom,
hip-swag: how naturally your walk sways
in kind. You are humankind,
my kind, kind to me, born well and gentle.
We believe in kind:
birth, origin, descent, nature,
sex, upbringing, race, our natural property,
so many things we naturally have
and have no need to struggle for
merely out of kindness to each other, or,
worse, to struggle for unnaturally.

Penniless Politics

A Satirical Poem

Part I

All politics the same crux: to define humankind richly.
No one non-populist or penniless can found a viable party
though most religions have such saints She was his Haitian
saint Emen – Emen for Marie-Noelle – for non-Christian
Mary-Christmas. In New York with him, her husband, Will Penniless,
they'll found their party in a poem. Black with White nation,
Voodoo-Haitian with immigrant Anglo-Scots, hairy-chesty,
penniless, Mrs Penniless, with him, Will Penniless.

To begin with everything missing. Emen set aside contempt
for extreme right or left, mein kampf or ill-kempt
politicians, or for middle-roaders. She held fire. 'If we got married
all might be overcome,' said Will hopefully, knowing their road
had to start absolutely from rough ground, not a track behind them,
just doves crowding trees black with starlings, white bird
between each black one. Their first steps aimed to pre-empt
mimicry of the past, to enter silence, then put it behind them.

Their poet has a white male face just as mean as each face
of rich white males in today's *Post*: the New York Mayor race.
So though he may tell he may not star in the story, outlawed
from penniless power. He (Will) tells how that day, bored,
Emen asked Will, 'Do we have to get married?' Who replied, 'For you,
power may grow by separation. But we whites are so flawed
that we must change sexually too. You decide.' 'For your race
I'll marry this once. And for love I'll make Voodoo for you.'

As Will and Emen tumble down through their love, he'll
keep telling their story impersonally. Sex needs such tact. They'll
always know she opened Will's eyes one morning in Brooklyn,
Utica Avenue; on their marital bed she, the Haitian,
changed his skin sympathies, unshackled his stiff pelvis
by mounting him, squirting black womanly sperm into him,
remaking his mind and his tongue while he was still
asleep, new conceptions warm and liquid in his pelvis.

The opening of eyes, changing of person, exchange of sexes,
Black for White, We for They, Woman on Top, all this is
not merely antithesis: lying on his back, Will gazed
up at Emen's eyes browsing as if he were a book while she grazed
his lips with Haitian lips, her hips working
at his hips, on his chest her breasts drifting cloudily sideways.
He felt male, white, but so much gave up his penis
to Emen that it could have been hers in him, working.

She sat above him on her altar there. Finished. Like her mother
once, a U.S. voodoo mambo retired to Ouanaminthe, crooning to Legba:
'*Attibon Legba, ouvri bayé pour moin,*' open the wicket
to the spirit world. '*Ago! Ou wé,*' you see me at the gate,
open it for me. '*Ouvri bayé pour moin, ouvri bayé.*' Hear
the call to Legba, Will, '*M'apé rentré lo ma tourné.*' Will wait,
'I will enter when I return'. Praise him, Will, '*Ma salut loa
yo!*' In origin male or female, red clay. Legba's old phallus here.

They talked of a Haitian memory: rare rains had caked the savannah
plateau as they travelled south from seeing maman
at Ouanaminthe on the Dom Rep border; they sat, stranded, shaken
by truck rides, beside the few huts, the Belgian mission
of St. Raphael, crossroads in flatlands, their rice and beans
bought fom a householder; in the backdrop each black mountain
patched with erosion's tarpaulins; this for Will a true Legba-
like moment, recalling Port-au-Prince slums, the kids lacking beans.

Under Nature's blind eyes, on Earth's body, Emen drew the congo cross
of souls circling criss-cross of living and dead. Heterodox,
Emen took a political vow with Will there, since maman mambo,
orthodox, had scorned their wedding, and added: 'I told you no:
I lived there: I was a *boat people* in a land of baseballs.
Her religion's Yankee politics. Mine's true to *noirisme*, voodoo,
My poor *pays terrifié*, suffering so bad from Papa Doc's
pouvoir baroniel, and now our poor make you country's baseballs!

'What matters,' maman had snarled, rounding the mid-pole of her *hounfor*
by the Massacre River, 'is hoe wide (*large*) you're thinking before
you begin.' Emen had made an oath: 'Let us live on the margin
of life and death, world citizens before our national origin,
unsexed before sexed, poor before rich. A great bowl fills a bucket
through a hole in the bottom, the world fills the domestic, women
fill men, magic fills the rational.' This world became what they swore
by the St. Raphael huts where 'wealth' was pink and slimy in a bucket.

Dawn there. Worrying burble of dawn chorus quietening. Dull.
A cloudy nowhere. Yet political. No sound now. Already political.
Pink light behind closed eyelids. In Will's blindness her brown hand
drawing a *vèvè*, the sacred figure, drawing with flour on to sand,
a simple cross on a St. Raphael path, white on brown, Legba
the Voodoo crossroads loa; in silence they were going beyond
pantheons and had trod out that single path to the simple
cross-stroke, first political choice, sign of Legba.

The *vèvè* scintillated at its cross-point, a glint of fire
issuing from an ant-hole in the inert silicon, a power
that transcends naming by priestcraft, not Allah's oneness,
nor Guatama's enlightenment, nor unity of trinity, nor singleness
at the heart of any four-fold-truth or of four ends of humans,
nor therefore finally Legba's own fire, nor a loa's prowess
but something obvious to all, a grand cliché: higher
knowing includes birth of action; at crossroads we become humans.

In the tiny flame's center the idea of their party was found.
Exactly in, not round it. They stepped inside there. Flames around
their embrace. Brotherly…sisterly…but also the sexual
flame inaugurates the political. Sweetened by flame they fell
down a chute of memory, partly personal but also transforming
the personal into memory held by whole peoples; central, central,
get central and you'll fall down that chute, flames, a dark
descent into conception, blindness of ideas transforming.

Beside Brooklyn's pale windows they reaffirmed Haiti, their apartment
a telephone receiver shape. Up on Utica, the brick tenement
looked downhill long past Carib cafes, bodegas, the Santeria
botanica where Emen bought plaster saints, down to shadier
Prospect Park; wind swept white doves off branches; starlings:
black dice thrown a moment. Trembling as if Legba possessed her:
'You've got to join my spirits before we talk of government.'
White doves skirting out in fear then flocking to the starlings.

Naked brown and whitey-pink, they walked through their apartment
on Utica and, arm round her, Will warned: 'You can't make government
from religious spirit.' The room full of charms, a St. John
statue at his knee, thunder loa stone, wall blankets, the Oshun
chiming bracelets beside steaming coffee. 'Political theory,'
she smiled, 'splits the world one way, and religion
splits it the other. We'll not mean more than we know and we'll invent
the unexpected, free of priestcraft, messianism, masculine theory.'

That morning they drafted their first manifesto, not in verse.
They looked in the jar: twenty dollars, a few cents, worse,
the phone cut off and a pizza to buy for lunch. Will put carbon-
layered sheets into his Olivetti and typed a little. '*Ah bon!*'
exclaimed Emen. 'Now add this, oh and this, and this,'
as the keys rattled and a fuzzy document emerged from the ribbon.
'Chain letters!' blurted Will. 'That will get over the curse
of poverty!' After retyping, the document read like this:

Dear Dolores:

The U.S. has room for a political party twice the size of the tired old Republicans and Democrats. Less than half the American people vote – easily the lowest turnout of any major Western democracy. Just add it up: 40 million missing voters or many more if everyone registered. A new political party could swamp an election. And it's going to be simpler to start one than you ever believed, so simple we're doing it by chain letter.

Photocopy this and send it to three or four of your friends – preferably ones who don't normally vote. Then come to the Memorial Day Center, 13th Street, on September 14. All questions about the new party will be answered then. We, the undiscovered political America, will make sure it's something we *can* vote for.

Sincerely,

EMEN and WILL

Take that prose and I'll… Let music take the prose and I'll
tell some real thing, giving the fictional melody and muscle
as 20 Hispanic and Black women bunch underneath the day
center's stage, 13th Street, and a massive Afro-Cuban who may
not stay, being the only male besides Will, and somehow does.
Emen at the mike says: 'Some of you think there's not so many
of us, but we only wanted 20 and thought probably female,
and here's a second man. Look at his size! He's tremendous!'

Emen sparked like static in her store-bought dress, gleaming brown
in buttercup yellow, hips perched on gold-painted pumps, downtown
strut across stage light shining from fierce excitement tight
and controlled. 'Yes, Mr Magnifico Cuban, *gwo neg*, you a right-
wing refugee? All *my* brothers sent back at sea. You get resident
status easy?' The man grinned like a bison. 'Just wanted to fight
for money, Ma'am. Ain't no professional fights on Cuba. I come aroun'
tonight to hear how you're goin' to give us our nest pee-resident.'

Emen: 'I'll name you now…name you High John, a long and knotty tap root.
Yessan my thoughts tie up in knots, my words'll untie the knot.
Listen to me girls, listen to me John, listen to me Will,
we're starting way in our minds behind the politicians. What'll
they do for us? D'you see East River swirling chemical
past our lives? White man sells a normal, sells a normal
condo: we're gonna drum a normal, drum a normal congo.
How does the song go? We all learnt it long ago
the hard way: ses sold on the corner, crack at Prospect Park.

Gonna drive through, senator? Don't stroll there in the dark,
shadow over neighbourhoods, your cartop movie
of clouds wiped black by bridges; coasting along, senator, groovy, poverty
only half visible, but evil all around. Do you get the vibes?
Car phone rings, another builder offering bribes.
In the toy war of your politics it's who has that ringing tone,
who gets stuck in craters sleeping on their own.
Behooooold this Brooklyn school, just trying to advance,
dirty feet itchy in old socks shuffling into the Regents
exam; and the school board dubious…
Does that make you furious?
Those politico horsemouths open and swallow the wind
while their high-rise projects suck our children
into elevators pungent with poverty. We're gonna put our sex
into estate management and City Hall won't guess what happens next.
You ought to see my new mind
new children alive there from microsecond to microsecond
and the wider winds rise in fury
us, us, supremely now the jury
sitting down in judgement on a loss of nationhood
we women with our bodies of light and blood
no longer on the doorstep making what we scrub
clean rise in price, no longer the soft-shelled crab
creeping into their kneeling buses, victims of the soft sell,
the hardness power of an exploding city. Well,
no law against making half a city highly moneyed
but we're going to make it spiritually honeyed
for behooooold the grim order reaper waiting for our lives
while lawyers and medicos store our honey in their hives.
Race, race, race, prunes supposed to hate the milk,
milk souring, greed, graft, greed, white talk
souring. We're going to eat Black food, my honeys, taste the snake;
we'll be Ayida-Weda's daughters; we'll take a trick
or two from Legba the trickster, even if you're Catholics
or whatever your sense of the sacred, you Hispanics,
or godless like Will, my husband dear, who tries so hard
to have dark consciousness though dressed in his leopard

sporty skin. As yet, don't ask me, we don't have a *program*.
Who d'you think I am? An economist, a law-maker? Don't be absurd,
High John. Let's put the serpent back in the sky. Politics
will come once we recreate spirit; then we'll talk *program*.'

High John thrust fist in air, captivated by the active haunches
of the buttercup Haitian striding there; he rode her vocal punches
with 'Awwight!'; otherwise grinned like a bear now, mute.
Fat and busy Dolores, at 50 unable to pay for her first heart
pacemaker, got irritated at male-ficarum and climbed the stage.
She fluttered black mackerel hue of Hispanic eyelids, her salute
fist contra fist to the Cuban, meaning 'You're out to many lunches',
as she said... but I'll enter her mind not her words at this stage.

I come over from Morrisania section, South Bronx, a bit
of Santeria here, Catholic there, great danger this room gets lit
up by flimflam. Don't be too smart: fool sees corruption
and hates the whole thing; police bad: hate policing; politician
bad: hate governing; monopoly stores bad: steal their produce;
until we live among and are thieves. City housing departments? I mention
'honest' up there I'm called naïve. I been pitching it
to them a hundred years; no result for puertoriqueño, can't produce

the *quid pro quo*, they say. D'you think my *barrio* don't know
'bout powerlessness? Morrisania, just tops for living below
the poverty line with income support, public assistance, 46 per cent.
plus,,,Medicaid, supplemental security: citywide only 17 per cent.
Vacant lots 39.1 per cent.; citywide 7.5...' Verna Lee Judge,
70, clearing wine bottles from the sidewalk.' The per cent.
of Aids deaths double the city's... Dolores spoke: 'You
gonna do a little *brujo*, little spell here or somping? Judge

for yourself, Emen. Who gonna listen? Sure, you look right pretty
up here, but try being dumpy, hunchback, chipmunk-eyed in this city
like me...' She grinned wide and whirled round to show her plump rump.
'You gonna take out full page ads like billionaire Donald Trump?
I tell you how to go to work. First we tell plenty lies, make trouble

until everyone say 'Hey! Whass going on?' We gotta bump
up the action, start us a little newspaper, get publicity,
dream a little trouble, make more, keep on troubling, no end to trouble.'

From the floor, Will: 'Our friend Dolores is celebrated
for championing her, er, *barrio*, Morrisania. But let's not get hated
like the city bureaucracy. We have to spread out from the, er, Tao
of immediate neighbourhood, of ourselves doing good, into
an honest politics engaged in the wider good. How can lies
be the best beginning?' Emen answered him: 'Put these two
views together, call the lies cheap tricks to get the poor started;
later appoint party honesty-functionaries to see where truth lies.'

Dolores again: 'It will need a few bucks to succeed with my plan,
for first this center's custodian needs a bribe; and then
you'll all go out tonight, infesting the neighbourhood with rumor
invented by me. Next, find me some trashy block newspaper
too local to know me, too small to check a freelance story,
and Will, you can rewrite my English. *The Brooklyn Blazer?*
Just right: only other editors read it!' It was the Cuban
who came up with cash; they got busy; so now read their story:

VOODOO'D VOTERS SWARM TO NEWEST U.S. PARTY

POLS WHO WORK BY MAGIC

The leaders of Spirit, a new political party, denied today that a Voodoo spell brought the public flocking to their first open meeting.

    A surprise turnout of 900 packed a small day care center in Brooklyn after attractive Haitian, Mrs Emen Penniless, daughter of a Voodoo priestess, sent out a single chain letter only two weeks before the meeting. The letter urged recipients to send further letters asking friends and strangers to go to the event.

    Bronx Hispanic radical, Dolores Esteves, charged that Mrs Penniless, well-known for her Voodoo practices, could only have raised such support by casting a spell.

'My envelope had herbs in it, and Emen's husband admitted that there were certain rites performed, though he wouldn't tell me what.'

Emen retorted that Dolores was miffed because her own years of activism had failed to draw the crowds. 'It's just plain tomfoolery,' she claimed.

She added: 'We are not a Voodoo party, but we respect the spiritual aspirations of ordinary people and think this respect is the missing element in modern politics.'

Spirit is aiming for the much sought-after 'third party' in the U.S. – the vast army of non-voters, whose numbers are double those of either the Republicans or Democrats.

Meanwhile, day center custodian, Giorgio Jacopucci, was grumbling: 'I wish they'd told me to expect so many – we nearly had a riot.'

The old chain letters would say, 'A woman in Syracuse
refused to participate and her house burnt down: don't you refuse.'
Despite your grin, some fear would seep in. To disturb
Spirit's electorate, the next letters had some harmless herb
dust in the envelope corner; and the chain began as before,
spreading links outward, down Long Island's great curve,
spattering into the Bronx, and to the Birth of the Blues
in NY, that's Harlem, and meetings were staged as before.

This went along with scandalous irruptions
into official occasions, such as the famous interruption
of the Nuyorican festival one August in Central Park,
when Emen, Dolores, and a horde of Hispanic women, stark
naked, leapt on to the bandstand and invited all men
to strip the secrecy off their masculine pride and mark
the festival with a vow to end male domination
of politics, reviving an ancient spirit between men and women.

Will himself, poet of the poem, was still the first non-American
convert, a non-franchised alien, a BBC-speaking Scotsman
who'd seen a bit of the world. He told them all
at a party gathering in Brooklyn that he had a call
as a Bard to charter their progress: he had a scheme
– since occasional arrests and constant publicity put them on

Page Three so often – that he thought would appeal to more intellectual
audiences: and NYCU were planning a lecture. Thus went the scheme:

A great writer from Africa was warming on sherry in the wings,
a voice they admired, the hall packed, when Emen and her sisterlings
mounted to the mike. 'We're the Student's Party for Internal
Righteousness and International Tolerance,' she lied, but with a kernel
of truth, for it spelt SPIRIT. Because she was so black
no Uni official dared top her: a photog from some journal
snap-snapped as Will joined her, 'Now listen to the things
this white man has written for those who aren't black.'

Will declaimed this:

WHITE CROSSROADS

'Ah'm to suck your asshole, stomp it,
aint mah style. You tell it, baby,
you tell it, John, okay?
This is the play-off boy, you know it, I know it.'

All the propertied amusements, whether
Leona promised Trump to sell her lump
of land, or whether Wall Street crashes
only temporary within the lifetime
of the dispossessed, it's psychological poverty
of tired whites with lots of balls
pretending to speak for heterogeneous nations,
sadly moral faces of governors, wizened
with the humor of getting their own way.

Even if their millionaire bridges are breaking up
already thin smoke lines
of the new bridges arc above falling girders
and Catherine wheel firework tyres
of phantom buses whisk across from City Hall.

*'Ah'm to suck your asshole, stomp it,
aint mah style. You tell it, baby,
you tell it, John, okay?
This is the play-off boy, you know it, I know it.'*

At crossroads mental crossroads multiply
down to City Hall of Cities Going Wrong.
So white Manhattan man woman white of sick tongue,
my white: my white shirtskirt, white of eyes,
newly arrived at crossroads of choice, as
white owner, leather attache box with locks,
moral owner manwoman me never could manage
Black bab bab voices crossing
smoked tarnish of tar of crossroads,
while Iyou white cross
to squash courts of whitened stainless steel,
fuckwords rising round us from legs
stretching out from walls. Me this
in other ways. Give up my plummy fucker voice.
Learn situation. Having left an English dream
half-finished, come abroad
seeking a voice change
to find that my voice must
crack open like a snake's egg for,
being its old self, whole and ineffectual,
it takes part in the real only by irony.

*'Ah'm to suck your asshole, stomp it,
aint mah style. You tell it, baby,
you tell it, John, okay?
This is the play-off boy, you know it, I know it.'*

My white life learns till middle age and stops.
Ask the white elderly what per cent
of their fellow world they've ignored.
Not too late in middle age to open out
to the Dahomey snakeloa, Damballah

the Voodoo-Santeria ordainer
whose red body wriggles along rainbows
whose venom spills yellow like egg purity,
the white skin of my life a container
of snaky kindship, moving in my moving limbs
across the crossroads, woman in me snaking,
my regard for myself priapic,
me, only a stranger, without a right,
willingly drinking righteous venom
until white face becomes suddenly spotty,
along my lily forearm a white wart,
my eyes discoloring and seeing new colors,
vomit on the street like a yellow ochre city
seen from a satellite, not without beauty
in these Cities Going Wrong.
On a stoop a bar of soap, White barges Blacks,
a dropped neon tube explodes into argument.

*'Ah'm to suck your asshole, stomp it,
aint mah style. You tell it, baby,
you tell it, John, okay?
This is the play-off boy, you know it, I know it.'*

Voodoo's lower Attibon Legba
cannot rule my crossroads of white indecisions
but protects in my dreams the black crossroads
and protects thresholds of new lives
writhing with the principle of the snake.

Below Will the hall seemed a tray and the audience its sweetmeats
in ranks: their silence another of poetry's defeats.
But the African writer swirled out in her highly-hued dress
from the wings, beaming and gently applauding. Quite shameless,
the intellectuals awoke to clap. Alas the stewards were already on stage
and Will and Emen spent the night in jail. Their arrests
reached the *Post*, page 3, 'Caught clambering over the seats'.
Though Spirit, as party, was mounting, no one guessed the next stage.

For with first success came first danger. They got too busy,
forgot spirit, spent on stunts, mailings, had the hypocrisy
to trade on their 'Voodoo Party' label, in *Post* headlines
became 'The Hex', while Dolores fed the *News* other lines:
'Non-Voters Anon', 'The Stunt Pols', 'The Slaughtered Chickens',
'The Spellbound', 'The Underdogs'; and they always met deadlines,
until in the party inner circle Emen spoke out: 'We're the Non-Policy
Party with a party machine. That's not how the spirit quickens.

The students have printed Will's poem; it's drawn in some scholars,'
Emen said, 'bibliophiles of the asshole, linguists of the followers
of the dollar. But you see my eye bruise?' (Badly swollen temple.)
'I earned this recruiting in crack tenements: it's all too simple –
with middle class white faces now joining our variegated force,
and their Press seeking copy – to become some Aime Semple
Macpherson phenomenon and forget we're the party for non-voters.'
At that, the silent Cuban, High John, revealed his own force.

Spirit'd had no suspicions of High John, monosyllabic, statuesque,
once a bit battered, baggy in suits like the dispossessed
he seemed to be. Maybe if he'd been more flamboyant a bruiser,
a notorious heavyweight, not a quiet cruiser,
the members of Spirit, mostly women, would have pierced the pseudonym
given by Emen. Instead, they'd written him off as a loser.
Anyway he'd been absent three weeks. But now a sudden unrest
by the door revealed him, Conqueroo, fists high to suit his pseudonym.

He came from the shadows to show them he too had an eye bruise
and a swollen chin. 'I don't s'pose many you women read the *News*
sports page today,' he said with his usual grin. 'And none you scholars
did's for sure. But this here's a cheque for 3 million dollars,
'cos I'm the new light-heavy champ of the whole freaking world!'
Pandemonium, rustle, newspaper sharing, until the Cuban's gappy molars
stared out from the back page. 'You've never asked for my views,'
said High John, 'but I can help your non-voters to win over the world.'

'Don't make me scales of laughter in this room,' said Dolores.
'What we going to do with this money? You, boxer, it sure is
everything we fight against you bring here.' But the Cuban replied:
'Okay. Capitalism. My big fist. Thump, thump. Right,
I read you, Dolores. But I have a little Capitalist housing plan;
most it is for the inner circle. And allow me this: we hide
the 3 million from the media. Can't fight slam-bam if the story is
you fight for charity. And I take a few risks in my hidden plan.'

This plan led to tragedy later with the party under attack:
the inner circle of Spirit were involved not with the crack
dealers, said a Channel 9 special, but with *Behemoth*, the new Ecstasy.
Emen didn't waver, for she strongly admired the Cuban, and I…
that's the poet…Will…suspected…that is, he had suspicions…
well never mind…For love of Emen and of Spirit, he swallowed a lie
in her loyalty and, liking the plan, fell not far behind
in backing the Cuban, even when fighting the most public suspicions.

For the time we'll keep the plan hush-hush, but High John staged
strict auditions for some kind of play. Even Will plunged
those with his rendition of 'White Crossroads'. 'Good, but not enough
courage,' chuckled his wife. Yet though she might laugh,
a sadness invaded her during the secret rehearsals: the cast
seemed to play various ghosts, an old crone, a rough
Columbian with stereotype Uzi, cops, and some part the Cuban upstaged
them all with; he looked reckless, as if his die were cast.

One day there could be other Cities of Spirit, and the model
for action will constantly change; for now, we'll tell of the ritual
that first made the party famous. Emen asked Will for love to dress
her one night as she lay down. He placed a finger vertical to bless
the wet rind of her glistening pubis, so's to seal in the love,
locate the political in the personal and spiritual, her breasts kissed,
a pallid mood lifting, nipples caressed, a radical
pair of panties covered with hearts slipped up with his hands of love,

twin-heart sex shop strapless brassière, a dress golden
and red with more hearts, symbols of the loa of love in the olden
religion, the jet ringlets gleaming on her brown skull,
his male lips in the hairy perfume, the final kiss from Will,
and then she dressed him with the same care. That night,
he rose high on stage in his cowboy boots and told a thousand people
that they would now see someone lovely to behold in
his eyes, the mother-like, the loa-like, Erzulie that night.

'We are the gods,' Emen told them. It was her new thing. 'Who are
the gods? We, we, we are. We are in train – ' (a rare
grammatical lapse in her oracular excitement) ' – We are in train
of creating a ritual, yes a ritual for a politics beginning again
in the breath of spirit. There will be a tunnel, there will be a mirror:
we shall pass through; there will be an altar: we shall attain
mercy before it; there will be a book: we shall write our
deepest thought in that book, over a cross, glassy as a mirror.

The cross will be on a tomb – Christian enough for you Christians?
I'll be thinking of the Voodoo family Ghédé, and you Buddhist nations
can think of the great beyond; and you atheists can just shiver;
but one thing we'll all learn by the ever-flowing river:
you can't speak true politics unless you keep knowing you're dying.
We'll resolve conflicts, yes, but that creates others. I believe a
tremulous sense of the sacred, a goodness that frightens,
wins our hearts fully when a friend lies to rest by that river.

And that's how we'll create policy, and they will call us the gods,
The founders, the neglected people who against all odds
Will bequeath their spirits to the future and will become the loas.
Now, I know that only I and some others have Voodoo, that most
have no religion or have other dogmas; this is not the issue,
for our nature is half spirit and this must speak so as
to touch the deeply inter-communal in humans, the lightning rods
of sympathy which should flash in each political issue.'

For a moment she sobbed softly at the beauty of thoughts
none can share with another, Erzulie, loa, in her courts
of love, perfumed with flowers, coquettish in a dance,
spinning round, showing brown thighs, wooing the audience
to the spirit of love, poignant. 'D'you tell me of the homeless?'
she sighed. 'I tell you of homes in your soul, a residence
there for everyone: that's where we build first.
No creation of policy if it's our souls which are homeless.

We'll plunder religions for their best, make off with spoils
– deadliest ceremonies, altar paraphernalia, and sacred symbols –
we'll set up wide areas, travelling temples made of wood
and canvas rituals of the dead turning to good
in white tents enclosing night on darkening river meadows.
They'll be 'art shows' to the park authorities but we'll be understood
by people of spirit, meditating there until the mind fails
and the soul speaks of policy in the tents by river meadows.'

By F.D. Roosevelt Drive, bordering the ungentrified
Alphabet City of Avenues C and D, the Lower East Side
has its playing fields. New York's Parks Department,
told of a 'performance art work' (though 'art' meant
here the art of creating politics) left them alone.
Each non-voter would meditate in a tiny compartment
then pass through a tunnel to a tent, there, ritually, to decide
what Spirit should choose were it to have one policy alone.

And so the party referendum began. At first it seemed absurd.
Down by the river on grassy wasteland at dusk (the word
already spread by the correspondence network, funds upcoming
from the Cuban), flatbeds trucks arrived amid a murmuring
crowd, a line of Portacabins went up, with a white tent central
and a wooden tunnel creakily winding towards it. Voodoo drumming
muffled on tambours. All on hire. Night fallen. Traffic heard
far-off. Otherwise silence. Non-voters in the cabins. The tent central.

Spirits sat down in darkness with their private mind,
these were party members squatting on stools behind
doors saying 'Occupied': they'd hired converted lavatories.
Lavatory, *hounfor*, cave, rushing water, wind through trees…
in isolation you can shed selfishness; shed
the pell-mell mind of self-interests until you find
your truest interest which you and others share. Rousseauist,
perhaps, but his citizens never squatted down in such a shed.

The faint urine smell was desirable; it anchored down
wandering thoughts; but as Mama Johnson for example hunkered down
in her shawl, on her stool, she, like all the others, saw
a photo of cemetery crosses glimmering on the cabin wall,
and, like all the others, heard a memory of voices in her head:
'Go be hard with men, chile, doan go be any more
hard with me, right? Liable pregnant her. Sank herself down
on ma sofa, stoned and risk of AIDS, just shit in her head.

'Shit, this place smelling of it. Did I tell you to watch the big guys
or what? I ain't talking to no Voodoo gods, but my eyes
shut all right, right? Praying into the heart of gold,
just like Emen told me, and I'm finding what? Old
Mr Pappy Man o' Mine, this heart finds you, this place
smells of piss. What's this? I see the urine trickling from cold
old bums in doorways, their blue black skin, slitty eyes
and damaged voices. My own old mama in that hospital place

'puffin at that oxygen tube, urinating in hospital, bare
black half moon ass, nurses wiping her drool, you doan care
'bout no politicky at the bed of death's for sure. Deep
things hover round her, come in your soul, doan quite weep
in your heart but get weepy for others' pain. I feel their power
in me now, working, that infected white baby next door, sleep
the last sleep, baby, with horrible blue black round your ear
spreadin' down your shoulders, I wan' you take my power.'

Mama began a travail of spirit, the eyes of her own dead
mother looking at her. This poet leaves aside as sacred
her hatred of wrongs to her race, but all other hates
flicked mothy wings at her mother's blank stare, twin agates
which still saw *her*, and the moth wings departed.
Still, male street talk bothered her ears. 'Jessie states
this, Sharpton that…' but her dead mother's face shuddered
with underworld breath, and finally all street-smart departed.

'These death things in me working. Oh, we can't put none that
right, right? Not the death things. But death's what we got
for to purify life with. Now *that's* politics.
Good protestant me, none them juju tricks.
Just this soundless dagger of death stuck in my soul
and this piss leaking from old men's pricks,
old women's pussies, makes me feel alive. Thrilled. I've sat
long enough now. I'm clear, clear right to my daggered soul.'

A half hour in darkness. Mama Johnson lived close to suffering,
but other non-voters sat for hours, their culture buffering
them from such clarity: that politics begins with the knowledge of death,
at a moment of birth, a moment of marriage, mid-breath
in the death of minds, birth of minds, sharing of minds,
measure for measure. They say until there was nothing left
in their thinking but the mid-moment, no false toughening
of attitude or wise cynicism, nothing but the sharing of minds.

A West-side lawyer came, scornful, and so spent two nights
encabined, wrestling with his demons, whereas three minutes
sufficed a Baptist minister, who opened his night's door and cried
'Hallelujah!' and so on, only to be mortified
when made to re-enter that darkness until he got kinder;
fast-thinking gays, closer than anyone to those who had died,
emerged weeping, and many failed and some started fights
when asked to retire; but those who voted had nearly all become kinder.

And we shall live in Ma Johnson's body, feel our stomach's weight,
breasts couched on it like elbows, troubled frown, heavy gait
swollen buttocks behind us under a print dress, an ache behind
our varicose knees as, feeling sombre, unusually kind
we climb out of our hut and tread damp, silvered grass to the tunnel,
where silently our people guard the entrance, a perfect mind
among us all, not our own. The wooden tunnel has a wooden gate;
the river gleaming across to Brooklyn; drumming in the tunnel.

Not yet a mass revival, this referendum, police car
flashing by the baseball diamond where a bonfire
lit the dancing, a line forming for the meditation,
a Haitian possessed by Ghédé – one form of elation,
the old East River in this spiritual, just a-rolling,
and Ma Johnson just a-strolling to the tunnel, proud in her nation
and in her body. 'I've got to keep my heaviness, my ugliness, entire:
that will light my fire, set the spirit rock and rolling.'

'Ouvway biyaay poor mwon,' was her password; they opened the wicket.
She mounted a ramp up to flat-bed trucks, set
at angles with others, bearing a 'tunnel' or rail wagon
bodies, gutted and linked together. Puffing, Ma Johnson
peered around in the close dark, smelt old food but saw nothing
in the tunnel's first leg until a low lamp came on
in an alcove, where sat a fat black man, top-hatted,
a dead cigar in gap-teeth, bright smile full of nothing

except banquet: plump cummerbunded stomach, gold-
timed shades, lawyer-striped trousers, and old-
fashioned spats above spit and polish toe caps. 'Ouvway
biyaay?' Ma repeated hesitantly. No reply.
He sat on, cross-legged, obviously a party member
taking part in a fun house charade, with nothing to say
as the lamp went out, the floor creaked like ice, cold
futures ahead, warmth in the past she'd begun to remember.

In a present of many choices, a hand tapping her shoulder
made her spin round in the tunnel. A bright diorama
like a florist's window lit up to one side
a vista of real roses, but after a second they started to slide
sideways as stage machinery rumbled and were nudged out of the way
by a panorama photo of graves. And who it was that had died –
whether her husband, her mother – she felt no one had told her,
and it would be herself one day, treading her graveyard way.

The short journey brought her to a final corridor
with a side table, two leathern chairs: an abandoned Pullman car,
a woman in white satin sitting there; she had a blue
stole, a sort of black Virgin Mary look, and she beckoned to
Ma Johnson to join her as she wolfed some wedding cake
beside a brass table lamp, her lips covered with goo
and her body breathing flower scents. Taking her place, Ma
nibbled, as directed, the sickly-sweet wedding cake

and found it falsely-happy opposite this wedded 'Mary'
who waited till she'd finished, then nodded, glanced away,
implying 'Now go'. (Unaware, Ma had passed an assessment:
anyone not solemn, any wrecker, anyone who offered harassment
in that car would by a trick of the doors be ushered
outside and calmed down by counsellors. Ma Johnson's embarrassment
was acceptable.) She rose and walked on, remembering the day
of her own wedding but wrongly: she a burlesque bride ushered

along a deserted aisle to marry that woman,
call her Mary, Emen, Erzulie, someone not quite human
but like her own soul. Down the corridor ahead
the exit now glimmered grey as all other lights cut dead
and walking towards the grey screen she saw an image
of herself approaching, waddling the way she had, a dead
spitting image in the same clothes, mimicking her every movement.
She passed straight through the screen, straight through her own image

as a curtain of silvered threads, that is, the 'screen', drifted
over her face and a whirring video camera clicked and stopped.
Suddenly fit for the occasion, Ma Johnson danced down a steep ramp
that led to a wide space of trampled grass, a damp
temple: overhead swooped shadowy wings of canvas
falling, skirting into walls; the dark air glistened, for an arc lamp
in the roof lit up a large mass on the ground, solid
wood that rose in black ledges; Spirit planned to canvass

political opinions on an altar. Now, this wasn't Voodoo
or the 'phenomenology of the transcendent self' – just a trick or two
for freshening up the normal, and Ma Johnson felt quite normal,
though she confronted a coffin sticking out of the altar: a funeral
despair and a hope of spiritual meaning transcending the religious.
The squared arches of many ledges formed a stepped mantle
over the coffin and each shelf bore icons, the Buddhas, the Hindu
figurines, a Koran, a menorah, a Toltec calendar, and not just religious

objects: a Humanist lapel badge, a philosophy book, 'The Sovereignty
of the Good' (for its title), activist posters, the rich plenty
of Civil Rights buttons. Above the coffin, dazzling on the altar,
lay a book whose pages were boldly handwritten. She felt a
fleck of water on her cheek as someone flashed out of the
shadows and sprinkled the grass with libations. They'd taught her
what to do next; so, whispering an oath to write down truth, and empty-
minded otherwise, she stepped forward, straddled the top of the

coffin and saw in its surface an embedded hologram: a white cross
seemingly swimming on blue waters, and at the criss-cross
was a hole like a mirror of waters, a depth we can sink
into, or from it dead souls may ascend if we think
of them as sunken. She moved till her knees were each side
of the cross now under her crotch in the darkness; she was a link
between upper and lower worlds; the book lay just across
from her on the ledge arching over the coffin, which from the side

formed the tongue of an altar-mouth, embedded with the hologram on which Ma squatted. ('Must write. Rest my goddam mouth,' she muttered. 'Momma up my middle. Or is it Jesus who is the Angel Mary? Or my ancestors rising from some underwater island? Scary feelings in my hand. Must write the three things Spirit must do.') She wrote: 'I never wanted much, just goodness. I wish we'd been happy. Oh but we can be!' ('Is that a thing? Okay then…') 'Make wealth,' she wrote and added, 'for others, for the children, anything we do

has to help the future and make our dead mommas and daddies proud.' ('Is that two or three? Well…') 'Stop the garbage.' She spoke aloud as she wrote: 'STOP ALL THIS GARBAGE, MA JOHNSON HAS
SPOKEN…'
It seemed so trivial, yet she felt the whole world had awoken as she looked at the book's instructions: 'Write the three things that Spirit must do. Turn to a clean page in this book and write the very first things in your mind. Don't be a coward about this.' Now Ma had done so; and these were her three.

And *Newsday* made it all clear:

VOODOO PARTY CASTS SPELL
– OF AGREEMENT

Spirit, the political party rumoured to act through Voodoo, claimed today that they'd found incredible agreement among the faithful about what party policy should be.

In a secret, two-month referendum, Spirit set up a funhouse on meadows bordering New York's East River.

At night, party members meditated in cabins, then walked through bizarre tunnels before entering a tent arranged like a temple. There, they straddled a coffin, and in a book resting on an altar wrote down their recommendations for policy.

'Call it supernatural or what, of the 1,000 members we had time to ask, 98% came up with an identical policy program,' said Spirit spokesperson Will Penniless.

'It's amazing. Once everyone's in the right frame of mind, we all know what a political program should look like.'

This was the program:

- Make material wealth for other people, spiritual wealth for ourselves. (Some, mostly men, specified that 'other people' meant the 'third world' or the 'homeless'. Some, mostly women, specifies, 'Help our neighbourhood first.')
- The only qualification for party membership should be goodness and respect for the history and future of the people's individual families.
- Long-term earth environment issues must have first consideration to save resources that our children's children should inherit.

Mr Penniless said this meant: 'Evidently not an end to the making of wealth. We can't help anyone without listening to the business lobby.' The point was to make greed go out of style, so that more desirable ways of using wealth result and that individual fortunes should not be amassed.

'Following one suggestion, we shall hand out year's suspensions – in a kindly way – to members who use normal political manoeuvres to destroy party happiness and decency.'

As for environmental issues, Spirit wants to confront popular opinion by cutting down on private car use, domestic trash and industrial waste. One voter just wrote: 'Stop this garbage.'

What about drugs and crime, and, if there's less of hydrocarbon pollution unemployment? Policing, rehabs, housing, international relations even – no real change in practical policies can come until the moral climate has changed, the party claims.

The Era of Dispute began. Marxists and anarchists, observing
the rise of the party, infiltrated meetings, noisily swerving
every debate into a grab for power. 'Power! Power!' –
'Pyuuhh! Pyuuhh! Emen would reply, pointing a pistol finger.
Church persons, too, sought to color all talk with their god. Spirit
politely asked some of these serpents to retire for a year:
then the slithery could come back on their own feet, deserving
to pass through the gate if they'd open their doctrines to Spirit.

Some non-voting students joined up and the agency newsman Peter Belia
(or Belly Belia', pronounced 'Memorabilia'),
brilliant, Blakeian, Zoa-like, jowls full of politics, T-shirt
of bottlegreen vinyl formed as if from leaves, pert
eyes with arched brows meeting in hooks. Leftist clichés
dazzled like coins on his lips: ozone, brokers hitting paydirt,
greenhouse effect, endangered forests, Nicaragony, Cubaphilia,
constitutional change, freeze on Wall Street dealings... But the clichés

made more than one eye gleam, for the great belly had swallowed
up Pentagon strengths on this missile, what House rules allowed,
who was deputy foreign minister in Burkina Faso – the Belly
had met him – who were Haiti's more notorious torturers, naturally
he'd met them, which made Emen shudder; above all he was expert in
the failure of American third parties, being himself a revolutionary
totalitarian who believed in the schizoid as authentic: few followed
him there, but some were impressed by all he was expert in.

He fell in the purges for decency, which gilded the party with fame
for the first time, as the Voodoo label dropped limply off and the name
became simply: pure Spirit. Belia nd his kind were a venomous
enemy if we're still talking Paradise. A second enemy was
an influx of white liberalism, of those whose own nation
did not live under day-to-day threat, and even your poet must
repeat that he lacks right to speak, yet must speak all the same
in honor of what he is not, of all that Baraka calls 'nation'.

For decency may also be dangerous: it opens the door for the brutal;
and while the deprived rage, it's there smiling, utterly futile
in its wish to be liked, to do right, to avoid discord, unease.
Yes, it rots the union of races it seeks; it's often a social disease
because it can't tolerate strangeness and mystery in others and secretly
it, too, seeks for power: as if they unengaged self, wishing to please
everyone, might also dominate them. Yes, nothing more subtle
than this enemy, which could survive these purges – but secretly –

– but secretly. The line's lame. The plot simultaneously sticks.
A poem gets stuck at a point; you can find it; the music is
always faulty there. Step back in the dance of the verse
and you see that the thought had already flagged, or, worse,
couldn't solve its problems. We were warned of this from the start:
'No one penniless can found a political party'; the poem stutters
to a halt at that point; the party not fully political, the public's
attention not fully caught. Go back; find the music; restart.

The music begins in each point over again, the beats that unite
the flow of melody into infinitesimal perceptions. And within each beat
the overall form is anticipated; so the past is caught up in the present:
the future breathes in the point. Here is the clue to the decent
founding of politics in a poem: that the future comes alive
now: that the neighbourhood is to the world as the moment
is to the whole; unlike the politicos, poets get their world right
if the point and the flow of the whole are united in beats: all alive

now and thrilling with the future. And so I look for the singer
who will sing the next part of the song truly. And I find her
making love: any woman. 'Our world,' she dreams, 'is shining with promise,'
and she spreads her labia for the pearled and purpling head of the penis,
while the man thinks: 'Point, point, penetrate right to the source
of time,' and she: 'Keep it moist with promise, for this
is our whole world weeping with joy, a gaseous planet, a voyager
through the ethereal to time's borders, pulsing out from the source.'

A Salvo for Africa

Our Family Is Full of Problems

A long, easy line of introduction, as if I'm a poet prosing alongside you,
a stranger, half-turning in his enthusiasms. We're in England,
descending the house-combed hillsides of Coventry,
early seventies, when the idea for these poems was born;
and we enter the shattered Hillfields suburb under the ring road.
I show you the surviving top shops,
terraces with wide upper windows blank in dark brick
where once the ribbon weavers' looms throbbed, driven
by a long, easy belt drive through attics of these joined homes
from one combustion engine in the end garden. Came the fall of cotton.
Came Second World War bombs, came socialist planners
bulldozing Hillfields, came the acrid fires of the homeless
on rubbled sites beside the high rises which trapped infants
in sweating flats far from their natural earth, families collapsing,
some crime – much exaggerated, some prostitution – from outside.
Came courage to live through a city's class and racial tensions,
scapegoats in 'Coventry's Square Mile of Crime'.
Now came the government again, with a full purse, to restore
the vanished community, as if money could replace the granny in 25
or the old man who played the spoons in 28, or the larger family
that was once the suburb of Hillfields. I turn to you, as if newly excited,
to explain how those planners implanted community centres,
went for mixed housing, sought to make a sunrise in the slums.
And created a middle-class boom instead. See the problem families
scatter as the suburb goes bourgeois. I point to the smart new brick.
See the hard truth of it: a free market nation will stick such families
right at the bottom; they'll never afford a house even one rung
above lowest and slip modestly aside from new building plots
into the next meanest doorway.

This relaxed walking – not a singing – gives us time for specifics;
but to see the problems of families puts a chord string of iron in the heart,
still there many years later in a country obsessed with free markets,
following the gleam of international power blocs, the EU, the WTO.

And I read a Daily Mail economist forecasting great wealth
for all free market countries. 'Of course, there will be basket cases,
such as Africa'. And I grab you by the arm.
'Did you hear that? Africa! Not a Coventry suburb, a whole continent
written off in our free trade fanaticism.' As if
holding your arm I face towards Africa and write these poems
as representative of a failed British imagination.

The iron chord is struck and I walk with you in Dar es Salaam.
In golden light move the stereotype dark suits
of World Bankers, planning, funding, organising, implementing,
evaluating corrugated sheets of shanties rattling in the sunny wind.
The government, lenient on forced eviction, has targeted
these slums for upgrading with World Bank funding
still in these early seventies; it will allocate building plots, slap down
fully-serviced cement foundations for squatters, a housing bank for loans,
providing you build to old colonial standards.
Low-income earners, the self-employed, the jobless
can't get these loans, can't build to such standards,
and the Hillfields, Coventry, story repeats itself.
The poor move out to new marginal, unserviced squatterdoms.
I follow them in my imagination and imagine I am following
the old slum-dwellers of Hillfields in Coventry
inexorably moving on.
Come the petit bourgeois, the middle classes,
come the slippery deals in land, till even the Bank admits:
'It is believed that many of the plots have unofficially
transferred to more affluent individuals.'
An inner city opened up to free market forces
will scatter the poor. World trade agreements blindly following
the forces that created a Hillfields are creating an Africa
ever falling behind this financial neo-colonialism,
the World Bank credo, the credo of the GATT, to help an Africa
bulldozed already by its own politicians.
Then I take your arm again and remark, 'I have risked prose,
a walking measure, to explain why I've written these poems.'

The Borrowed Bow

The moment stings, shorting like an old wireless
of bakelite body with a trellised raffia screen.
The shadowy corner's acrid with electricity,
blue air frazzed with black
in a cliffside house blank-windowed towards France.
But around the space of shock are other rooms
where old men, sitting by their wirelesses,
wear country check worsteds with a fleck of red
blodged with gravy. This moment
is a vanishing point on a post-war seacoast,
the pier blown up in case of German invasion.

The rooms still have that slow life
moving in them, a termite-gnawed Asante mask
on the walls of a retired colonial official,
an assegai from elsewhere in Africa,
a boot-polish shield, a bow, a poisoned arrow;
for there's an unexplored magic in all time,
a survival even now of a toothless mouth
sopping at a biscuit, a hand trembling
on a bony knee, about to reach
for porcelain on a frame of swivelling trays,
thin finger crooked as for a trigger.

I borrowed the bow of black hardwood,
took it and a bamboo stick into the garden.
Couldn't pull the leather string back;
the magic of the bow-spar wouldn't bend for me.
I knew I was just meddling. So I went indoors
to fiddle with the wireless innards:
electronic emotions and jerky excitements
in the village of valves, which cracked like gunfire,
a tracer arc streaked across dusty connections,
as if before the snap of it, the coil of smoke,
a tiny bow had shot a brilliant arrow.

The Childhood Map

An Africa the size of a British park
cracked like a white map,
a manageable terrain,
or coloured in with adventures
for boyhood dreams of the bush,
brown and sere, gazelles,
scouted by cheetahs on their hills,
streaming over the high plateaux
of Kenya beneath the fuselage
of a plane that lands long ago, lightly,
into history. In present time
it could only land tourists,
and it's worse than that.

Locust aircraft turns on its wire arm
lands in a toyshop window. Trembles.
Child minds excited but blank.
As adults, we are reading
liberal history books:
the oily tones of the Whitehall elite
with their city interests and ties
setting up Kikuyu Home Guards
to fight Kikuyu Mau Mau.
For every white man killed
four hundred Africans killed.

Toy planes still landing long ago.
Kenya gripped by one-party rule now
its opposition enfeebled.
If Britain were beset by famines,
would it be governable?
Shining pupils of our aristocratic schools
rise to well-fed pomposity
of managing nations

of making the EU competitive
against boys running ragged
down river banks in Nairobi.

The toyshop window lights up again.
A slender plane with medicaments
or is it a white human body
is flying low over Africa dispensing
a fraction of western money spent on AIDS:
HIV truck drivers in Rwanda
say, 51 percent; Uganda
36 percent; Kenya who
knows, 19 percent; commercial
sex workers in bars
34 to 88 percent –

the stanza
breaks apart, Africa
cracks like a painted tin landscape
in a child's small attention.
Elsewhere beyond this window
its greatness breathes like a leopard.
Will these statistics never be finished?
Can we never get on the right side of them?
Watching our little plane
on its slender piece of wire
land behind the window.

The New Medicine

Three leading London hospitals have completed all the routine treatments
that the authorities had provided for that year.

Hospitals too productive, come to the end of their budgets for ops,
routine surgery halted till the next budget, way of the world would mean
some bag lady didn't get her op, the bishop got his
with medical insurance like all higher-ups
on the internal market for organ repair.
Bank clerk not pushy, only a gristly testicular tumour, probably not him,
Wasn't he nearly sixty, had to wait for a specialist, no big problem,
Actress got her ovary op and a lot of attention in the media, bank clerk who?
He didn't die, you know, not him, these are not sentimental matters but
                                                            bred in
the bone morals that what we do is sacred to each other, fat
chance. Baby mine, in memory, covered blue-black with staff infection,
nurses dabbing with calamine lotion, joking the sweetest jokes,
as the black invaded your neck.
What if those nurses had been infected by profit?
We have the money, you know, no problem. Baby, in memory still,
writhed on the bed, skin of a certain mottling, dried mackerel skin.
What if the baby ran into debt?
Should have looked where they were running when they voted for
                                                            the bastards,
half a nation.
My mother voted for them, didn't look, had a mastectomy one time
but laughed when I said she had one breast in the grave now, and
medical insurance,
took an aneurism later, very cheery woman,
cheery being almost the highest moral gift because it beams outwards.
Price plays a part when the State chooses your hospital
no one gets the best without paying.
Nurse came to you, mother, like my conscience,
cool and neutral, warm and smiley, not like my restless individualism;
she built your body up in bed like a cornucopia riddled with it, conscience.

Have you had your medicine, man? said she to mother,
and I think of African lands where illness was a communal fault,
and witch doctors beat out psychiatrists in curing neuroses.
Oh but Britain's our medicine man, dying of its own accord.
Sometimes there's nothing to lift the heart from the death bed.
No grand causes left to fight for, said Osborne's old play.
But that's when the one cause becomes huge and obvious,
seen in the amused astral focus of the death principle:
our lives no more important than our deaths,
but by god you'd better get them both right on line,
no jumping the queue to live,
no pushing others forward in the queue to die.

The Toe of a Continent

The toe of a continent has been dipped into hope
while the body is covered with slashes and bruises,
the little countries gaping with wounds:
Liberia savage in wars where once was freedom;
Freetown ideals spent out in Sierra Leone;
Rwanda entering history as a monument
to genocide, to French interference
and inter-tribal blindness. The centre
of Africa ravaged. After the murderous
dictators, the torture cells, the hard-hearted
arrogant coups, the lie of the single party,
its necessity never proved;
and the brilliant leftists, proud
to invent solutions, shunting their people
into co-operative villages and into worse poverty;
after euphoria of independence
used to create power for bloody-handed soldiers;
after the panicky flight of white money,
the desperate loans, welcomed at first
at over-high interests, never a gift,
but the banks piling debts on drowning nations;
then after the closing of banking privileges,
after it all – the cadences of Auden –
after slaughter of families –
we can never imagine the scale of it –
desperately we imagine a river of hope still runs,
and the Northern banks will respond.

At the foot of this poem lies South Africa,
dipped into hope, where traitorous whites
have already started shifting our money,
and global investors withhold their starter funds,
but where Mandela, untrembling,
his toe in the black river, waded deeper

into hope for this whole continent,
like someone finally baptised into a faith
more equal, more ancient than Christianity.
Who will provide such a priceless balm?
What industrial nation, able to pay
a part of the sum, will end our betrayal?
How slowly evil plots in darkness
away from such rivers. How quickly
South Africa changed when it changed.
How little the poem can know.

Well of Sorrows in Purple Tinctures

These thoughts in purple knots of cloud
dash down false lightning flashes like
neon signs above the glistening
Grands Boulevards, illuminating streetwise
melodramas not without beauty when
the will grows weary of the nightlong life
and you go walking.

I keep returning to Paris from scenes of death;
each time a problem with the plumbing
lets out the teary waters.
Plumber came to plumb my flat
on the rue des Messageries just now,
disjointed the pipes behind the bath tiles,
refilled the ancient well of sorrows
dried up since the baroque years,
drenched Boehringer's ceiling down below,
his concert office closed at Pentecost.
A frog with immense white limbs
swims in the well.

And I'm walking with a gospel tune in mind
which Eddie sent over from the States.
Says life's a burden you can lay down.

Lay my-ah
burden down, go walking
go walking on the other side
of the Grands Boulevards;
neon silently barks at a pigeon
sends it up in flurries like a bat;
let it rest. See my-ah
dressed in his golf leathers
father there,

see my-ah
dressed in white hair
mother there,
see my-ah
dressed in her Pentecost
sister there,
see my-ah
dressed in stained feathers
baby son there.
No side on the other side.

See my father falling on the fairway
of his life. Light goes out,
but darkness won't descend
on featureless houses,
absence of mood,
golf course grass greying and serious,
the whack gone out of the game,
the blood gone out of the brain,
trees coming alive with night
but not releasing it.
No passion yet in this childhood of a thought.
Past time's a heron once
in the course pond:
straw leg dislocated in water clear to the bottom.

A lot is loaded down, settled for good.
But who's uneasy there no more?
Who's in trouble there no more?

See my mother lay her head,
flakes of soap on a transparent pillow
an empty memory fringed with lace
(the snow fell
on such a resting place),
an elderly woman lies down there
dressed in her last cardigan,

in her coma,
the watery pillow whirls with lights
and heart-beat oscillography blips.
I will her soul to go if it wants to.
"Please go, wherever you are."
It flurries upwards like a white bat.
Who took the soap flakes packet,
let the flakes float down?
I was thinking of Jean Cocteau.

Emotions stagger forwards
in these distracted counsels.
I turn my head:
a gate had fallen away in her face.
And I continue walking.

See my sister; when her mouth was
morphine-dry, God sent saliva,
so she could sing her valediction hymn.
My-ah burden down.
Her belief a fixed acquittal
in the *cause célèbre* of our lives,
and I had thoughts on another side
of my mind. Mine the pale legs
like a huge white frog, went swimming
off Grenada's Grande Anse jetty
in the Caribbean Sea. Journalists floated
round about; it was thunderous
night above truffled green waters
welling onto beach of palm shadows.
Dressed in stained leathers,
a bat flew low on the wave, up
sidelong through a lightning flash
and I was hot shit in that flash romance.
Back in Surrey there
saw my sister who revealed her face
brimming with mysterious fortune,

the face of one who justly assumed
in her dying that she'd earned a heaven.
Something very God-like rose within her;
she was immeasurably superior to me then,
interrupted the purple lightning.
Bade me goodbye from her armchair;
I withdrew with a curious grimace.

A lot is loaded down now, I say,
halfway become my nature.
And I go walking on the boulevards,
bail à céder, soldes,
a price is no price unless a sale price;
my elbows are itchier than in the old days,
each time in Paris I'm more settled in habit,
a journeyman of innocence:
behold this Faustian innocent
shedding deaths of others
as he goes walking.

See my baby lay his head on a down pillow,
pigeons flurrying on the boulevards.
Lay my bird in down.
Well, Tom's long in his coffin, inside his altar,
in some cathedral I've made for him
lit by summer photographic flashes.
I scarcely dare cross those cracked flags.
Why do I see instead the electric figure
of a black abbot
flitting along the galleries like a bat
and into high doors?
You'll never know where he'll appear next
in these galleries of my unbelief.
I don't know where the abbot is now,
for I'm casting the deaths of others
like disjointed stones into the cathedral well.

I continue walking towards what remains.
The trail I have left is the trail left behind.
On this, my third time of living in Paris,
I know these memories as
the mere same endroits;
the voice that used to speak for me is still there,
but I'm learning to speak over it, catching
it up like an under-air
on the Grands Boulevards,
pigeons high against empurpling clouds.

Arrondissements

The Shattered Crystal

A Little Night

A word to come lies in a little night
where ash is falling.
The word can't be this "coffin",
lying in its candour, in its cinders.
Inside, the poet's too lazy in his death
to perform a truth singly. All's ambiguous.

Yet a coffin is blocked in boldly, I see,
under the washing down of night.
The cobalt blue cabinet's cut on a slant
with candelabra making mirrors
along its sides peopling it with mourners,
delegates from the governments of poetry
and from their industries, who appear
only as reflections of shoulders.
Hostility of moths round the candles.
Hostility of mouths still saying "coffin".

The coffin waits in this little night
for the whole day's train.

My own face, visible in the mirrors now,
is a bruise again floating in hints of crystal.
I don't *yearn* towards my shadow, bowing
to it, reaching out to find lost unity;
for if the shadow really touched my finger
untruth would constitute truth, whereas
as Buber knew, the process takes a *Thou*.

Our shadows lack performance;
they are a text created by the dusty mirror;
I do all the touching and my finger

returns with its ashen tip, as you
the reader, when you touch these unreal ashes
find your own finger-tip is clean.

In our candour to be truthful, we're very stern
and talk too much of loss, covering our truths
with ashes – like authoritarian fathers
who damn their sons with an over-strict word.
"You'll never amount to anything".

The word I care about
(it's been lying inside the slant cabinet
wakes and now performs itself:
The word becomes "Celan", formerly Antschel:
the only poet I have to struggle against
because none wrote more beautifully post-war
of the perfection and terror of crystal.

The Weekend Curfew

After the weekend curfew Celan
found the house
shuttered
the parents in captivity
himself condemned
to being enemy of himself.
His *Todesfuge*
began. Later that lyric
was, for many years,
an urn carried in German
ceremonies of forgetfulness
disguised as memory.
And so
Celan smashed it
with his intellect's hammer.

For Nazi cruelty in its purist light
had filled that lyric,
a vessel of the Sephiroth,
and when the hammer broke it
musical fragments
became shards,
part of the song went hiding
silent in stones,
dark rising past the
secretly-glowing
stones on ashheaps,
words that
each whip
stroke cracked open
in savage light.

And we, we'd emulate this,
letting our lyrics croak
the throat
into broken music
as if mere self-unease
were our righteousness
smashing the lyric vessel
in darkness
so to be as smart as he was
oh to be as smart as he was
our words nowhere near bursting
with such a lesser weight of light,
as we flip through
the fragments
of our cheque book stubs.

Evening Descending Mauve: Gisèle Celan-Lestrange

Evening descending mauve
on the rue Montorgeuil,
presenting on the palm of the sky
a navy-blue bruise,
and old Jewish wound,
not a nail-hole.
I go calling on Gisèle again
in my mind,
to thank her for a New Year etching
of rocks that were almost rain.

Her face with its knowledge of suicide,
her low voice and cancer-death
easily haunt me now.
I had a skyscape in her pastels,
half-owned by a friend,
six months a time on our walls;
its troublesome clouds
were also rocks bruising land.
Now her life seems a diptych to me
of joy and fire one side,
the other, later, side mauve
as prison camp snow.
Her husband Celan's
early poem to his parents
shot by the Germans
takes on new meaning:
"You didn't die the mauve death"
(of cyanide gas).

Shocked by unsuspected absence,
I return on the straight road
past Heine's lodgings
to my fishcarter's faubourg.
Gisèle calls me from the outerworld

– once the call was real,
but this is the haunting –
and I half-hear her lovely reply
to a chance remark at dinner
on the Montorgeuil. I'd told her:
"A poet's suicide may
for a moment cut the path
of the past to the future."
(because there is no bridge
across its dreadful river banks,
though the path one day reforms
after so great a life
as an Iris bridge, yet of stone too).
For a tactless moment the room
became her husband's grave,
in the far wild water a file opening.

While I live Gisèle calls me
frequently to say,
"*Ça m'a profondement touchée,*"
taking part-ownership in the remark,
so that I become moved
by the iridescent bridges of Celan
and of Celan-Lestrange

Crystal Eagle 1
(In Memoriam: *Paul Celan*)

A crystal eagle tied by the neck
with soft silk braid, like a unicorn
restrained by a virgin, sneers
and draws in snow crystals of its breath
when I move my head to make lights
travel along its beak. There's future
silence of the non-forthcoming in the rue

de Paradis shop window – rue
de Paradis once the près-des-filles-Dieu.
Villeroy & Boch have laid five glass hearts
around the eagle plinth, gold-amber,
lemon, red, blue, purple, whose bruises
slide within the under-wings. Myself
a stranger at home in this widowed
Jewish crystal quarter, I muse
on a suicide that I can't in all decency
address as *tu*. But if I could,
the silken braid would fall, the eagle
rising, draw a chariot through the sky
towards mauve snow around a throne,
centre of all that's celestial in Celan.

Light in Back

The streets were blasted by road works.
Tar mazes, black cravid, flame skirts,
stimplumzitt of tar damper, sear ooze
(the two-word stage of acquiring poetry
from some complete moment), wild it with fa,
grossly about ambition, excess lipid,
try vivid, or limpid, try vivid, yes vivid,
make lold. In their moment those words
anticipated sorrows like the people
lost to us in our future, a vanished race
of tall skirts dressed in old altar cloths.
I can't hand on poetry while it's in
this state, widowed by words I married.

Sun buzz had made the windows
grey with dust on the rue de Trevise,
that street noise, alive, began fading,
as twilight fell. *Hear, O Israel* was shut.

An old man's torch wobbling its beam
around the bookshop's far back room;
torch beams fringed his beard of truth;
in the window, minorahs and bechers.
My eyes travelled on from ritual objects
through the word to his light. Make lold.
We can't remain windowed by words,
Must intuit origin. And so this past
Immediately becomes news to hand on.

My poorly-made road's good only
for a word-created world, a glued-together
alphabet sphere spinning in bluish plastic.
I'm lonely of it. But I thought-created
a lot of worlds in the space before this one,
as I stood at the rue de Trevise window,
my words about to begin in already faded
yellow air above the road machines –
a possible million of worlds in their lumps,
or luminous imaginings, red shifting,
uninformed by languages, *en voyage*
to the harlequin light of beginning
terrifying or utterly quiet.

From rue d'Enfer to rue Bleue Again

Heaven and hell obviously split-mind stuff, like
laying the same on the same, blue doubled on blue,
yellow gulping up in laughter to the skies, or
black and fire on black and fire, with reddened anger
burning at the bottom. Heaven is happiness
multiplied by the infinity of the instant, blanked
off from Hell's anger-fear trapped in its own
blind instant.

In this intense mood, I try to see inside
the cat box that Schrödinger left in a car
outside Heine's house where I cross the road
as usual and go for croissants on the rue Bleue.
No sound comes from the breathing holes.
It's not the animal that's dead but thought itself
trying to make the opposites of life or death
interpenetrate.

Here's a shop on the rue Bleue that sells brass
and only brass, long rails of it, door handles
and a measuring counter in the empty spaces.
That's same on same, but only like habit, like
having your coffee every morning with the croissant.
To see brass and then again brass, forever
staring at the same brass plate in the shop window,
takes you within brass.

And seeing piano wood and again piano wood takes
you within all tunes pianos might play. I turn
into the boulangerie where the croissants
bite each other in rows. That's just crabby habit,
repetition of detail. The smoothness of brass
is easier to see, same on its same, than rough pastry.
And a manic emotion takes you inside itself and then
inside itself again.

China Blue

Chinese Bridport

Then the morning shadow falls, suddenly slanting
down monstrous apartment blocks at Porte de Choisy
and its Chinatown, over a piazza of pagoda-style
kiosks. Diaspora money with its huge fist
has thrust buildings into earth here, cliffs of them
with mud-coloured balconies and strata of pallid walls.
Knocking from his heights, an Asian fixes a lathe
and he knocks at my heart till morning shadows slant
again down Bridport's cliffs, an early time in England
by a calm sea, a place to start poetry from.
Everyone hurries across the piazza; there's push-chair
after push-chair, new growth, and a man spits
dangerously over the head of the baby he's wheeling.

Money in Sunshine

for J.H. Prynne

Jeremy, marvellously tight in your word orders,
your lines never run on endlessly like this huge
rectangular high-riser; though, if the sky's blue,
it sharpens into a classic. A pigeon flights
along precipices, past shrubs at balcony levels.
Peregrine falcon. Downstairs, a window
mumbles in Cambodian and higher up
glass swivels inwards, holes in the bedazzled.
After immigrant hardship, families come
to this excessively sublime wall of flats:
an escape from sewing, their children at it
too; they've saved harder than I could; bins

in the malls filled with cottons, male underpants
for a pittance; the female have vestigial lace,
go baggy in the crotch. Chinese speculators,
whose raw energy and care I admire, stretched
these balconies on too long, wanting a luxury
to gaze at. It's like a poem with a word order
betrayed by volubility, money destroying
the limits of syllables because it won't stop
talking until all the profit is squeezed out.

Calling Them Home

Lost ones of no shape behind the shudder door
of the side-street music shop displaying
Nouvelles du Cambodge. A winter leaf
enters on the heel, though Paris skies
are summery enough in Chinatown.
'Pol Pot, organiser of genocide, is dead,'
the news-sheet announces. To lose
your family in the wider passing-on
is process of life but not when memory's
vertebrae lie shattered, so the music
store owner sells the paper reluctantly
to a foreigner whose mind is klutzy
with Europe-Asie. No bell tinkles
as the shop door closes but a quick drift
of sparrows across the avenue draws
attention to a coal-tit in the Metro foliage,
its black poll, white nape, and call of if-he.

Transcending the Hypermarket

Heavy meat smell by the cheap
chicken counter: the birds sell
too fast to be displayed seductively
but pile up in a massacre heap.
Only the adept know that content
drawn carefully into a single
blinding act of mind unites
its contraries, simultaneous
but in all possible orders.
Birds packed separately
under the glass sales counter
by palm slaps can only unite
closed eyes with dry beaks;
mass squirms with evil, this
loose skin twisted unbearably.

Fidelity

Fidelity to family's a fine thing,
but fidelity to knees?
So are you my pal, dog,
in the Chinese hypermarket?

Well, there's a niece in New Zealand,
brother's child boyfriending over there,
and I'm sniffing around in Tang Frères
on the avenue d'Ivry, where
durian doré pods from Thailand
are a green (not gold) giant's
prickly bollocks.

Three Cambodian fingers lie
on a sales counter,

the other two hang off:
that's my three in the cemetery,
we two brothers still dangling.

We need fidelity to family
when the family's wrong
but not fidelity to wrong targets.

Inland shimmering
in the grumpy aquarium:
the fish are calling for the vinegar
of their final swim in soup
as they mope about or poke about.

I have nothing to buy the even money
on our odd chance of disappearance,
hand through the water
that plucks us up.

Outside, a thysanopter
probative of heat – shit! –
why didn't I say 'an insect
with fringed wings proved
that it was hot and steamy?'

Sunset dribbles reds on glowers,
strips of squid whiten in chopsticks
held to the last light
above tables on the street.

East-West Apartments

You turn a corner, come upon it, the thumping,
suddenly two tunnels divide at an angle-point
of choice; it's a figment in black cotton, very

shaky indeed, a small man with a claw-hammer
nails up a franco-oriental friendship notice in a warren
of flats spiced with fingers and curries. You've
turned and come upon heavy sweat; thudding blurs
into thumping going both ways down the corridors,
a spicy line of doors with Chinese lintels or
an empty Catholic room of white school tables.
He goes a bit slippery, avoids choice with two notices,
each in its language, each to a wall. This man
is a cunning man, taps nails in the slime between
tiles, not that discipline of murder: comradeship
struck into the vertical angle itself like a club
shattering the nape at the human point of choice.
This thumping follows now like two heart-beats.
Whatever they say, keep loyal to friendships in
France, Britain, U.S.A. Hit hard the kick button
when selecting the Devil and you'll fight using Angel,
or go a bit slippery and hope those old friends know
that you've posters in several different languages.

Puppets in the Buttes Chaumont

Water. Right. First. In a park botched up
from a plaster of Paris quarry. Sovereignty of
a dinky mountain island rooted in gypsum,
rather Chinese, and topped by a fake
Victorian pagoda, the cliff bluffs reflected
as broken parmegiano cheese in immobilised
depths. You know it's foreign when the birds
are wrong, a mandarin duck writing under
ripples disturbs some cross-bred thing
with white mange. Your eyes follow a gnat
and flick to the rocks where a jackdaw bullets up
towards the highest bridge, a kite being flown
in the clouds up there. Everything writhes

with the false as if parasols could walk
along cliff parapets into the artificial caves.
Water darkens emptily, the rockface loses light
in serious transition. A fleet of Vietnamese
puppets comes to float on the lake and mimics
the insensate ducks: an emperor with a palanquin,
his tiny boats pulsed into cradle motions
by poles of puppeteers working half-submerged
behind screens. Again the gaze lifts to the mountain;
the setting sun highlights a mysterious bridge,
wedged into a cleft, a yellow embroidered top
to a grey shirt pocket. You've taken your pen
from your own shirt: dusk begins to unify
all that's synthetic though you're forced
to use it genuinely. So you send the clouds,
as if you were a Chinese poet, off to distant friends.

Château Noir

(for Allen Ginsberg)

Turning from Cézanne's Château Noir
gardens, peaceful in blades of intense paint,
I move to the Orangerie's windows. It's
breezy; and that's a tree and that's a tree,
in a regular line down the Seine;
the straight strokes and ferocious white
streaks on the current measure out
river prosody by durations hung in the
airiness of attention rather than flowing.
Towards this come oars which sip
at memory: was it the Cam at Cambridge,
racing hulls sliding past foliage, blades
that dip into things precious? While here
on Concorde they go along among the trees
(I mean those French figures in their hurries)

towards bluish mists of the river-run; I've
not read their futures yet; they, unlike me,
seem to know where they're headed.

Might as well go down again to the basement
where the old head-slam of Monet's water lilies
renews thoughts of Cambridge: our pram
with nylon pillow frills stood nearly in the river
shallows there as crews raced past. In a flick,
the oars vanish and I'm back in France.
On Monet's powder-blue waters float lines
above depths and two curving tree trunks,
stranded at the sides of the painting,
bracket my eye-span, so nothing measures
out these inner depths which are very still,
though anything but peaceful, being vertical.

Notes

Oppo Hectic (Ferry Press, 1969).

'When I Was in Bridport', *Resuscitator 2R3/4*, February 1969;
'The Earthen Stairs', *Collection 3*, January 1969;
'The Furnaces', *The Anona Wynn*, June 1969;
'Oppo Hectic', *Collection 5*, July 1969;
'Ordnance Survey Map 178', *The Park 4 & 5*, Summer 1969;
'Mongol in the woods':
'The autobiographical story moves from 1969, when our Down's Syndrome baby son, Tom, died, an event that permanently changed the way I view my life, politics, and, curiously perhaps, prosody'; Preface to *Selected Poems* (Talisman House, New Jersey, 1996); sub-note to the Preface: 'My unredeemed use of the term "mongol" reflects usage in the mid-1960s and I have retained it, therefore.'

The Diagram Poems (Ferry Press, 1979)

The prose introduction, 'Night Shift', appeared in a revised version of the text printed in *Kind* (Allardyce, Barnett, 1987). The text is as follows:

NIGHT SHIFT

If any urban guerrillas tried not to deserve the label "terrorist" is was the Tupamaros in Uruguay, savagely put down by the military government of the 1970s. Apparently, they were the Robin Hood revolutionaries: they would kidnap a banker's son or an ambassador or make some lightning raid but always remained considerate to the general public. We used to get their stories on the English Desk night shift at Agence France-Presse in Paris; they would be wired through by AFP's local stringer, translated into French and English by the subs, and the next you knew the story would be sold on the streets of news-voracious Tokyo: orchestrated by the Spanish-speaking Tupamaros for maximum heroic effect, transformed into a French news story, into an English news story's very different rhetoric. And finally into the columns, say, of the *Asahi Shimbun*, in whatever rhetoric the Japanese use.

    At HQ you were in the middle of the news-making, but were not a pure element of transmission. You were a little drunk from a visit to "Les Finances" on a corner of the Bourse, an all-night bar, now demolished, where the fearsome Marionette would serve her favourite journalists before attending to more dubious night-time clientele. Back upstairs in the large foreign-service room, you'd look at the Uruguay copy, try to understand happenings thousands of miles away, and simultaneously might be thinking in a maudlin way about a son who'd died two years before, or about the difficulty of political judgement. This, too, entered the occasion of the story for you.

Uruguay itself, the poverty caused by the crash of world wool and meat markets and by local and Western financial interests exploiting the native population – a nation's history lay behind the agency cable. But whether the guerrillas were right or wrong, you were dreaming quite obliquely, as you tapped the stories out, of how an authentic politics might combine the mildness of your dead baby with the stern wisdom of a judicious elder minister: some beneficial balance, instead of revolutionary flamboyance and a dictatorship's response of iron rule. Only a fool, while ill-informed, supports anyone else's violence; so political judgement was suspended: it was held at a distance by a screen of words.

That year, the story of the Tupamaros' "Operation Pando" came to me, once more in French out of the Spanish, but now in a book written by the guerrillas in their own high rhetoric, which I pored over during the intervals between stories. In Pando, population 15,000, they seized the police and fire stations, the telephone exchange, and three banks before trying, not too successfully, to escape as one of the world's more notorious police forces closed in on them. The aims were to grab weapons and money, to bring off a propaganda coup, and to open a daring scope for Tupamaro activities. Operation Pando was, in fact, the beginning of the end for them.

I began drawing diagrams to see what the guerrilla movements looked like on paper, and I made notes (rescued from an old file only the other day), letting fantasy deepen till something in me – no matter what – pierced the screen of words and answered to the urgency of Operation Pando. The poems that came from this cannot be pure: they begin in the guerillas' movements and in the notes made about them, before reaching their own imaginary landscape, singed by the real.

—'Team Leader': revised edition opens with prose introduction:
Cars needed: they hire funeral convoy from Montevideo to Pando cemetery – getaway rendezvous for all teams. Undertaker's men neutralised.
Small boy, nearly hit en route *to Pando, is called 'imprudent': with this word, all the following heroics begin to lose innocence.*

Team leader should have been given scooter, with comrade has to steal car. Late to check assembly points and targets. Shots already at police station. White handkerchief signal to start.

Opening lines of stanza 1:

> Must be getting on,
> though the fantasy is moving.

—'P.C.': revised with prose introduction:
Police Station: reconnoitred on previous visits for licences and papers. Same dog taken twice to be vaccinated.
Now the teams call in casually: two "sociologists", two "car accident victims", three "airforce officers".
All goes smoothly until Sgt. Oliviera bursts out of dormitory, fires, disappears, reappears in central patio, shuts himself in dormitory. Then surrenders.
Police who enter the station are captured and, with those on premises, placed in cells.
British airforce tomtit blue…

Last two lines of Stanza 3:

> a sickening English insouciance
> for anything beyond island sympathies.

—'The Fire Station': revised with prose introduction:

Firemen might warn Montevideo or police next door: a tannoy is by the fence. The Tupamaros' account of capturing the firemen tries humour: "He pisses right down to the last drop and finally turns round. He regards Roli who is holding him up with a gun and yelling insults. Then, without appearing in the least surprised, he lazily raises his arm, as if stretching. What apathetic men these firemen are!"
Meanwhile, police and crowds on the streets outside the fire station. An old man comes through the crowd and places boxes on pavement – parrot-like bird suddenly flies out of one of them.

—'Central': revised with prose introduction:

They have to cut off the telephone exchange.

A pregnant woman has a nervous collapse: is cared for.
Across the road, old people queue for pensions, children bustle into school. One comrade guarding the street "thinks about the children who will have a much better life than these poor old people."

— 'Arrest': revised with prose introduction:

Bank of the Republic, largest: the police increasingly a problem.
Teams enter in three groups, the last containing a false policeman who disarms a real policeman snoozing on a chair. Van with three comrades and seven captured funeral firm employees outside.
Fake policeman has fun – with popular approval – controlling the crowds. In the ban a comrade is accidentally wounded when a colleague picks up his fallen armband. Raiders escape in overloaded vehicles. One comrade does not hear the evacuation order, is pointed out to the police, and arrested.

—'Gold': revised with prose introduction:

Pan de Azucar bank, smallest. Perfect operation.
They capture a man watching too closely and take him next door to the Pando bank; likewise a trembling policeman. But a mother and child are sheltered. They take money and the manager's car.

—'U': revised with prose introduction:

Pando bank, second largest. Comrades in position, leader calls out: "This is an attack. We are the Tupermaros." Another leader leaps on to the U-shaped counter, brandishes an automatic weapon. Comrades range through bank, including a basement saferoom where private valuables are kept. A worn Luger fires twice, harmlessly. Comrades take in the two prisoners from "Gold". Trouble in streets, a siren wails, they leave.
Exchange of shots with policeman in the street. Flat tyre. More shots, en route, *with another policeman and a bystander is wounded as he leaves a bar. Escape car collides with an obstructing van before, windows broken, it limps off to the cemetery assembly point.*

—'The Diagonal is Diagonal': revised with prose introduction:

At cemetery, "funeral cortege" gets under way, hearse leading. They drop off protesting funeral employees.

After two traffic policemen try to stop it, cortege divides and the hearse and two cars escape to Montevideo. The other group turns left and one van stops to collect a waiting Gutbrod truck which they load with money. One car continues, only to run into a police ambush by a bridge. Five Tupamaros leg it across the fields; the two remaining guerrilla vehicles arrive. Roadside gun battle. Eight comrades wrest Gutbrod round and ride off to hide money in a prairie.
Back at Bridge, 20 guerillas, including three women, stumbling across fields to woods; split up into smaller groups. Sirens on all approach roads; helicopter; police. The account claims that in various incidents the comrades are killed or captured and mistreated.
Last diagram a diagonal path. Vicious events burst over a ledge of violence like a slanting waterfall.

l. 14 'cloacal pool of suffering'
l. 17-23 It was the Tupamaros' Operation Pando:
    I now name these incidents
    so many years after
    they came to me at night in a busy newsroom.
    Yet let me not lay claim to them
    for I little own this poem; it is nothing
    without the original movements.

l. 35 exactly is the cemetery

The Infant and the Pearl (Silver Hounds, 1985);

Author's note to the first edition:
I should like to direct attention to stanza 3 of section XVI, from which it is clear, by extension of argument, that no real politicians either appear or are attacked in the dream: only the phantasmagoria that flit across the world of the media and float into our subconscious.
  The metre is based on that of the late medieval poem, 'Pearl'. The prescribed extra verse (let us say a return to the sign of unity) on top of the form's 100 stanzas seems most naturally placed at the end.

A later note added by Oliver to his *Selected Poems* of 1996 (Talisman House Publishers):

This poem follows the prosody of the anonymous medieval classic, *Pearl*, with a few tricks to lighten it for the modern ear.

Rosine appears in my work here and elsewhere as representative of a natural, non-doctrinal socialism. Margaret (which means "Pearl" in Greek) stands not for Margaret Thatcher herself, but Mrs Thatcher as presented to the electorate – at the time when the poem was begun she had recently won the first of her sweeping electoral victories. She already appears in the 1973 novel, *The Harmless Building*, as a personage ironically of potential greatness.

The dedication is to:
Jan, Kate and Bonamy.

An Island That Is All The World (in *Three Variations on a Theme of Harm*, Paladin Poetry, 1990);

Penniless Politics, A Satirical Poem (Hoarse Commerce, 1991, reprinted by Scarlet Editions in New York, 1992, revised for Bloodaxe, Books, 1994); *Dedicated to the poets of Lower East Side, New York City, and to the community of St Mark's Place, who showed me much kindness during my nearly five years' residence there. I never said I didn't love New York.*

A Salvo for Africa (Bloodaxe Books, 2000);
The sequence of poems constitutes Book I of *Arrondissements*, a series of books on themes arising from life in the arrondissements of Paris.

'Well of Sorrows in Purple Tinctures' published in *Arrondissements* (Salt Publishing, 2003);

'The Shattered Crystal', *Arrondissements* (Salt Publishing, 2003)

'China Blue', *Arrondissements* (Salt Publishing, 2003)

Alice Notley's editor's note to *Arrondissements*:

Shortly before he fell ill with cancer, Doug decided to make a single manuscript of *The Shattered Crystal, China Blue*, and *The Video House of Fame*. Since he was hurrying to complete *Whisper Louise*, his final book, he didn't have time to see to the last details of the present manuscript.

He left no indication as to its overall title; there were still decisions to be made as to the final choices for *The Shattered Crystal*; and he apparently wanted to include a preface taking off from his preface to the selection of poems, called "from *Arrondissements*", which appeared in *etruscan reader viii* (edited by Nicholas Johnson).

I feel I have no choice but to call the book *Arrondissements*, though the project Doug referred to as *Arrondissements* also includes *A Salvo For Africa*, published by Bloodaxe, and *Whisper Louise*, a double biography, in prose, of himself and Louise Michel, as yet unpublished.

I have also decided to include the poem "Well of Sorrows in Purple Tinctures", since it is an important poem and fits into no other context. It is a natural lead-in to *The Shattered Crystal* and to the present volume. Doug seems to have envisioned a collection of individual poems as part of the whole, but "Well of Sorrows" is the only one I'm certain of as belonging.

Also included, below, is the preface from *etruscan reader viii*, outlining the *Arrondissements* project.

As for the selection of poems in *The Shattered Crystal*, I've opted for the most inclusive presentation offered among his papers.

Preface

A poet of modern Paris has to write about more than the river mists fogging the Pont Mirabeau while Apollinaire's river flows beneath.

As in any major capital these days, whole districts of my adopted city have dense concentrations of individual nationalities; to name them would be to name much of the world. In my own district, straddling the 9th and 10th arrondissements, it's the Jews and North Africans; in the Goutte d'Or (19th) the francophone Africans; in the 13th and 19th the Chinese, Vietnamese, and other Asians; Americans are everywhere; Brits and other West Europeans crowd into metros; White Russians have been long established and the collapse of East Europe has brought in waves of new immigrants and gipsy beggars too; the Indians and Pakistanis have a restaurant alley; there's an Australian pub and several Irish ones while Haitians and other francophone Caribbeans and Latin Americans have their own cultural centre. And there's the French…

For those in love with the myths of Paris as the Gallic City of Lights, cultural centre of the world, there's poignancy in these changes, as the National Front has not been slow to realise. But for a poet, it's as if this excitably-proud city has at last reached its maturity.

More than mid-way through my life I have begun writing *Arrondissements*, a series of books or long sequences in poetry and prose, designed to reflect the world at large through the prism of Paris. I investigate these arrondissements until an idea comes for a piece of writing suggested by the nature of the district. What follows is a sampling so far:

'Well of Sorrows in Purple Tinctures' is set in the Grands Boulevards of the 2nd arrondissement. It is part of the collection called *Miscellaneous Poems from Arrondissements*.

Whisper Louise (in-progress) began at the site of a 19th century ballroom in the 20th arrondissement The book centres on my own memoirs and those of Louise Michel, so-called 'Red Virgin' of the Paris Commune, the short-lived city rebellion of 1871. (Théophile Ferré was her platonic love, a hard-line revolutionary executed by firing squad.)

The Shattered Crystal is a sequence of meditations on the poetry of Heinrich Heine, Paul Celan, and, a little, Sully Prudhomme, all of whom had connections with my own district, Faubourg Poissonière-Montorgueil (10th leading towards the 2nd).

China Blue is a shorter sequence on the Chinese/Vietnamese/Thai/Cambodian/Laotian diaspora of the 13th and 19th.

The Video House of Fame takes wing from the video arcades of the 2nd and 4th arrondissements.

A Salvo for Africa (published by Bloodaxe) is a book reflecting from a purely European perspective on the future of Africa; the theme was suggested by explorations in the 18th and 19th arrondissements.

Since I have little control over the process by which these books come to life, I deliberately refuse to decide in advance what genre to adopt – whether more broadly accessible or more tightly experimental, whether located in self or more decenteredly. This can easily be misunderstood. I have abandoned none of the avant-garde's long fought-for positions, nor its current interest in verbal density and texture, nor my loyalty to its practitioners. But the avant-garde is always, in hindsight, a genre. The *Arrondissement* project keeps obliging me to cross stylistic borders. Our minds, after all, have many genres of activity, and the genres of life found in a great city surpass our mere individuality to an extent that no one approach to writing can match.

Douglas Oliver

www.ingramcontent.com/pod-product-compliance
Lightning Source LLC
Chambersburg PA
CBHW022011160426
43197CB00007B/377